Heritage Breeds

Berkshire
This, the most popular of the heritage breeds, yields a bright pink meat that is sweet and creamy with a hint of nuttiness.

Duroc
A hearty and somewhat aggressive breed. Duroc pork is known for its high moisture content and rich flavor.

Gloucestershire Old Spot
A critically rare breed with a gentle temperament. Gloucestershire pork is known for its higher fat ratio that adds a juicy rich flavor.

Hereford
Resembling a Hereford cow in markings, these pasturing pigs have a calm disposition. They are slow growing, yielding a richly marbled and colored meat.

Large Black
A critically rare pasturing pig with wide shoulders and a long body. Its short muscle fibers and ample bellies produce moist meat and exceptionally tasty bacon.

Ossabaw
A rare breed of small-range pigs with a heavy coat and long snout. This breed has a high percentage of healthy fat and darker red meat that makes some of the best charcuterie.

Mangalitsa
Known as the "Wooly Pig" for its wooly coat and hearty disposition. This breed is known for its high-quality lard-like fat and super juicy, flavorful meat.

Red Wattle
Gets its name from the red color of its coat and the fleshy skin that hangs under its jowls. Prized for its tender meat with a rich beef-like taste and texture.

Yorkshire
The pigs of my youth! Yorkshires are hearty pasturing hogs and the females make wonderful mothers farrowing large litters of piglets.

Tamworth
A smaller athletic hog with a reddish coat and an ample belly. Tamworths produce the very best bacon.

The
Whole Hog
Cookbook

The Whole Hog Cookbook

Chops, Loin, Shoulder, Bacon, and All That Good Stuff

Libbie Summers

foreword
by Paula Deen

photography
by Chia Chong

RIZZOLI
NEW YORK

New York · Paris · London · Milan

*For Joshua and Anthony,
my merchants of marvels
and peddlers of dreams*

First published in the United States of America in 2011
by Rizzoli International Publications, Inc.
300 Park Avenue South, New York, NY 10010
www.rizzoliusa.com

© Libbie Summers
Photographs © Chia Chong
Foreword Text © Paula Deen

2011 2012 2013 2014 / 10 9 8 7 6 5 4 3 2 1

This book is published in conjunction with the celebration of the 75th anniversary of
Smithfield Hams. Whenever you see this symbol , it means that the recipe was
developed specifically for the Smithfield product indicated.

Design by Jennifer S. Muller | Illustrations by Arianna Stolt, uglygreen.com

Edited by Janice Shay, Pinafore Press

Printed in China

ISBN: 978-0-8478-3682-6

Library of Congress Control Number: 2011927159

contents

Pigs are my favorite animals by a long shot. I love to cook pork, and of course it's always featured on my menu. But there's more to this animal than tasty trotters. Pigs are smart, curious, industrious, and resourceful. In fact, now that I think about it, they share all these fine traits with my friend Libbie Summers. These two are the perfect match for a fabulous cookbook—and I can just hear her hooting with laughter as she reads this!

Libbie and I have worked together for a number of years. She is presently the culinary producer for my network shows, as well as the senior food editor for my company, Paula Deen Enterprises. We have barrels of fun working together because she shares my love of Southern food, she's terrifically organized, I can always rely on her, and we both have a wicked sense of humor. She is able to add a gourmet factor that elevates each dish she prepares. I think that Libbie's world travels have given her a vast store of food knowledge (in her former life, she was a private chef on yachts that sailed around the world). She incorporates this know-how into all her dishes.

In order to talk about Libbie's food presentation and the wow factor she brings to her dishes, I need to tell you something about Libbie: She has style, and she ain't bashful about showin' it. In her choice of clothing and jewelry, she likes to mix high fashion with eclectic, vintage things. Even her dog wears a pearl necklace. The combinations are always fun, and we look forward to seeing just what outfits Libbie will wear to the set each day. Her job as culinary producer is behind the scenes; nonetheless, she does like to entertain. This creative instinct is one of the reasons I trust Libbie with all my personal catering needs. If I give a party, Libbie will be designing the menu as well as the table settings.

Of course, Libbie looks out for my boys, Jamie and Bobby, too, working on recipe development for The Deen Brothers Enterprises and handling culinary production for Jamie's show. I can truthfully say that Libbie seems a part of this family, since she has shared her culinary magic with us in so many ways.

A true and informed love of pork has led to the compilation of this wonderful cookbook, featuring recipes inspired by many different cuisines around the world. I'm gonna bet you will enjoy the West Indian Pork Roti, Asian-inspired Pulled Pork Spring Rolls, and Hot Peppered Pickled Pig's Feet from the Deep South as much as I do.

In fact, I have had the pleasure of tasting many of the recipes in this book, and I recommend them all. With the choices in this cookbook, you have all you need to plan the main dish for an important dinner party, or you can simply choose to make fun snacks to nosh in front of the television. Last Christmas I hosted a very large open house, and Libbie served her Scottish Quail Eggs for me, which are hard-boiled quail eggs rolled in a homemade sausage, deep-fried, and served with a special tarragon mustard sauce. These tiny, tasty eggs were the perfect finger food and the definitive highlight of the party menu, as far as I'm concerned.

Memorable food. That's what Libbie shares with you in this delightful cookbook.

–Paula Deen

It started with a spanking. Really just a gentle tap on the rear, but enough to startle me, since my grandma Lula Mae reserved such punishment only for truly criminal offenses. I hadn't done anything to warrant the spanking, or so I thought. You see, my cousin Pam and I had tried to ride one of grandma's prized Yorkshires bareback. The louder that pig squealed, the harder we laughed. Lula Mae rushed out to the field to see what all the commotion was about. When she saw us terrorizing her pig, we expected her to laugh along with us—maybe even try riding him for a few seconds herself. But she didn't laugh. She didn't even smile. Instead, she shot me a look that made me feel like I was skinny-dipping in an ice-cube tray. Apparently, you don't ride your grandma's prized pig. I had never before seen her this angry, and I never saw her that angry again. But at that moment, I stood there humbled. I realized my place in the pecking order. That was my first lesson in pork appreciation. There would be many more.

With my grandparents, it wasn't about holding Heritage-breed bragging rights. The pigs they kept on their small farm in rural Missouri were essential to their survival. My grandparents watched over their pigs with the kind of reverence usually reserved for holy things. As a child, I couldn't understand what all the fuss was about—every one of those pigs would eventually meet its destiny on a chopping block. But as I grew older and watched Lula Mae hover over the butcher, insisting that no scrap of her esteemed pig be left on the floor, I began to see the honor in respectfully raising and preparing your own food. She cooked every portion of the pig—from "snout to shitter" as she used to say—which sometimes called for a great deal of culinary creativity. Liver or trotters, for instance, just don't sauté and pickle themselves. The best dishes begin with fresh, high-quality cuts and are topped off with a healthy dose of ingenuity. Watching my grandmother transform a large slab of pork belly, pulled from the bowels of her rusty meat freezer, into an imaginative meal for ten people certainly helped to inform my professional cooking career. She was fueled by necessity. I am fueled by the challenge.

My professional culinary career began many years ago when I was hired to cook for silver-spooned owners and guests aboard private sailing yachts, traveling the world. Cooking for an eclectic group of celebrities on a boat that in rough weather is sometimes nearly lying on its side requires not only a calm temperament, but a steady knife hand. I'm told I have both. But onboard cooking poses a number of challenges that extend beyond a hard-to-impress clientele and troublesome seas. Even the largest sailing yachts have limited refrigeration space, so the ability to source and use fresh local ingredients from each port of call is a necessity for any yacht chef. For me, it's both an inconvenience and a welcome challenge. I've happily MacGyvered inspired dishes out of very limited resources—often what was being sold that day from a farmer's wagon on the side of a dirt road. But at each port I made a point of acquainting myself with that culture's people through the common language of food. I've gleaned soybeans from a nearby seaside field and roasted them for a cocktail party snack, and purchased goat meat so fresh I swear I could still feel the heartbeat as I carried it back to the boat. No matter how many times you try to tell people how important it is to eat fresh local ingredients, it just doesn't resonate with them until they've tasted a gyro made from a slab of pork belly from a pig butchered just moments before being cooked. Refrigerating this meat was not always an option; to freeze it would have been an insult—to waste it, a sin.

Over the years I've made an art of creating inventive and enticing dishes from what would often be the castaway cuts of the uninspired chef. I liken it to playing dress-up. Some dishes call for a finishing touch, as a coat, hat, scarf, and gloves complete an ensemble—similar to covering a pot of chitterlings in hot sauce and vinegar for a finishing touch. And others just need a flirty skirt, like my Jerk Roasted Tenderloin with Banana Chutney. There's really no place for prêt-à-porter fashion when playing dress-up, just as there's no excuse for making "safe" recipes when we have access to so many wonderful flavors—even on small islands. Sure, barbeque is good, but add an over-the-top Hot Guava Dipping Sauce to my Ribs St. Barthelemy, and you have "couture cuisine."

To push the metaphor further, few mass-produced products can compare to the unique, handmade items that are gaining in popularity and accessibility, like those found at weekend farmers' markets. The distinction isn't necessarily the price—it's the quality. More often than not, when these local artisans employ good practices, good products are the result. The same applies to the way we produce and consume our food. As it turns out, our ancestors were on the right path with their pig-farming practices. You see, my grandparents' pigs were liberated. They were allowed to roam freely and forage for food at will through the rich Missouri woods, resulting in happy pigs with robustly flavored meat. Pigs are what they eat—and to think that we're any different would be fooling ourselves. So consumers are starting to take interest—asking questions and demanding choices.

On the heels of the current trend to provide consumers with the variety and quality we are beginning to desire, artisanal pork producers are popping up across the United States. Their emphasis on sustainable farming practices informs how they go about raising Heritage breeds. Knowing your Heritage breeds is like learning to distinguish between sushi-grade tuna and the stuff in the can—clearly, there's a difference.

The Berkshire hogs are the most popular of all the Heritage breeds. Berkshires, black pigs with white legs, produce a somewhat brighter pork with a sweet, nutty flavor. The Red Wattle, with its red color and fleshy skin that hangs under its jowls, is prized for tender meat and top-notch hams. Red Wattle pork is lean and juicy with a big beef-like flavor and texture. The Tamworth hog of Ireland is a smaller breed, recognizable by its reddish coat, upright ears, and long snout. They are known for their sizeable belly and are considered the best bacon hogs. I can attest to their quality, I once hiked for two miles with 20 pounds of just-butchered Tamworth hog belly in my backpack during a cruise through Ireland. The King's Belly Sandwiches I served the next day after a long, slow braise set the bar high for the rest of the cruise. The feral breed of Ossabaw Island hogs are originally from Spain, but landed in the United States just south of my current home in Savannah, Georgia, on Ossabaw Island. They are extremely rare and have a very heavy, hairy coat, and a long snout. Ossabaw Island hogs have a high percentage of healthy mono-unsaturated fat and make excellent charcuterie. Large Black hogs are true grazing hogs and perfect for "pastured pork." They are a docile and friendly breed with short black hair, wide shoulders, a long deep body, and a penchant for belly rubs. Their ears are large and hang forward covering their eyes and most of their face. They are aptly named because they often weigh more than 700 pounds. Large Blacks produce excellent bacon and moist meat. Finally, the Magalitsa hog is known as the "Wooly Pig" because of its characteristic thick wooly coat and its ability to withstand extreme conditions. It is a rare breed and is often said to be the Wagyu of pork because of its high percentage of marbling (double that of average pork), which makes juicy, tender meat that doesn't shrink up when cooking.

Armed with this information, you now have the luxury of being selective. But let's be honest. Let's be real. Not everyone has access to a corner butcher or a farm that boasts Heritage-bred and pasture-raised organic pork. And that's okay, because you can still buy exceptional pork from a family-run business at your local grocery store. In fact, you probably already do. The well-known Smithfield Packing Company has been a trusted American pork producer for 75 years. Started by the Luter family in 1936, Smithfield has become a worldwide marketer of pork products and one of America's largest meat companies while still retaining its family Heritage. And you don't even have to wait in line to have it packaged up.

Becoming a thoughtful consumer who is mindful of what you're buying and eating means knowing the origin of your pig as well as the cut of meat on your plate. By now, we're all becoming familiar with the term "primal cuts," those large cuts of meat initially separated from the carcass during butchering. Within *The Whole Hog Cookbook,* I'd like to take it one step further by familiarizing you with some of the retail cuts that are broken down from those primal cuts and, more importantly, explaining how they are best prepared. Take the Boston shoulder, for example. Cuts from the upper portion of the front legs of a well-exercised pig tend to be tough. Makes sense, right? But that doesn't mean you should avoid these cuts. In fact, because they contain a good amount of fat, these cuts are ideal for slow roasting or using a braising method. With a little ingenuity and a couple of hours of slow cooking, that once-tough shoulder can become fork-tender succulent.

While you'll learn enough about pork in these pages to earn you a spot on *Jeopardy,* that's really beside the point. The purpose is to empower you as a cook. To give you the confidence to ask a butcher for a double rack of pork for a pork crown roast, but the guts to stop him before he trims and ties it—because the step-by-step "How To" in this book will give you the courage and wisdom to do it yourself. To encourage you to put down that package of premade breakfast sausage and buy a fresh pork shoulder instead, so you can try your hand at making your own sausage. To challenge you to create a special seasoning for your sausage that will become your new "family secret." Just try. Be fearless. My friend the pig is forgiving.

My grandma Lula Mae, however, was not. She never really trusted me around her Yorkshires after the rodeo-riding incident. I suppose, in some ways, this book is my way of letting her know that I get it. Food isn't just something we stuff into our mouths when our stomachs growl. With some thoughtful and creative preparation, mere food can be transformed into heart-warming sustenance. These are the principles on which Lula Mae's kitchen was based. It's what inspires my cooking today. I harbor no resentment or jealousy toward those pigs Grandma protected. Because in the end, I know what side of the chopping block I'll be on.

–Libbie Summers

tied tenderloin

ears

belly

rib chops

★

Retail Cuts of Pork

★

ground pork

jowl

feet

back ribs

whole fresh ham

Boston shoulder butt roast

spare ribs

hogmaws (stomach)

hocks/shanks

backfat

fresh sausages

picnic shoulder roast

rack of pork

1

Loin

| blade chop | butterfly chop | loin chop | rib chop | country style ribs |

| sirloin | back ribs | top loin roast | tenderloin | blade loin |

| center loin | sirloin cutlet | porterhouse |

loin

Cuts from the loin are some of the leanest, most tender, and (usually) most expensive cuts of this still very affordable meat. The loin of the pig is the long strip of tender, lean meat located between the leg and the shoulder on either side of the spine and on top of the ribs. It includes both country style ribs (which are not really ribs at all, but are the cut from the front end of the back ribs near the shoulder of the pig; country style ribs are more meaty and less fatty than back ribs, and should be cooked by the same method as chops), back ribs (connected to the backbone and nestled under the loin muscle), and chops. Because of their mild flavor, pork loin retail cuts adapt well to a wide variety of seasonings and sauces. The phrase "high on the hog" refers to the superior cuts of a pig that come from the higher parts of the pig's body—the back and upper leg. English aristocracy feasted on the fine meats from "high on the hog," while peasants ate from the lower sections of the pig.

Cooking Methods: Best cooked using dry heat, although chops are best braised, pan-broiled or pan-fried.

Colossal Pork Tenderloin Sandwich

This is trashy Midwestern eating at its finest. You could be on a back road goin' nowhere, comin' from nowhere, and haven't even been anywhere, when all of a sudden you would come upon a roadside dive selling this tenderloin sandwich that was so big and so divine, you'd give up your virginity and your only ride home just for a bite. Men have sold their souls for less. Clearly, I'm not talking about some average-Joe pork sandwich. This tenderloin is pounded thin, dredged, deep-fried, and sitting on a glob of mayonnaise, ketchup, and the cheapest bun you can imagine—all pale and tasteless, taken separately. But put together, this sandwich is something you live for.

I first came across this sandwich when I was ten years old. I was staying at my grandma's farmhouse, and she promised that if I stayed out of her hair and kept my nose clean, she'd take me and my cousins on a trip into town in her pickup truck (kids and coon dogs in the back), and get a bite to eat. Like most kids, up to that age I begged for Ding Dongs and root beer floats, but after Grandma bought me that first tenderloin sandwich, it was all I ever dreamed about. All day I'd be trying to be as good as I could—keeping my cussing and complaining under my breath—just to get my hands on that damn sandwich.

It didn't disappoint. One sandwich could feed four people. The bun looked like it belonged on a slider compared to the size of the mammoth tenderloin that sat on it. That delicious hunk of meat was pounded out and seasoned just with salt and pepper, but it tasted like angels had kissed it. I can remember the ketchup and mayonnaise running together like a pink river down my arm.

Unless you're from the heart of Illinois or Missouri, you might never have experienced anything like that tenderloin sandwich, and that's a shame. So I'm including it here because I wouldn't want you to miss out. In my recipe, of course, I up the ante. I make a mayonnaise from scratch and describe a real Butt-Kickin' Ketchup that will pretty much blow your mind. One you will want to keep in your refrigerator at all times.

You may not be a Midwesterner, but there isn't any harm in eating like one every now and then.

Colossal Pork Tenderloin Sandwich (page 18)

Colossal Pork Tenderloin Sandwich

butt-kickin' ketchup · entrée · serves 4

Peanut oil for deep-frying

2 cups self-rising flour

1 teaspoon kosher salt, plus more for sprinkling

½ teaspoon freshly ground black pepper, plus more for sprinkling

½ teaspoon garlic powder

2 large eggs, beaten

1 pound pork tenderloin, cut into 4 equal pieces

4 sandwich buns (the cheap kind)

Homemade Mayonnaise (page 80)

Butt-Kickin' Ketchup (recipe follows)

In a Dutch oven or deep skillet, heat at least 4 inches of peanut oil to 360°F. Line a baking sheet with paper towels and set aside.

In a shallow baking dish, whisk together the flour, salt, pepper, and garlic powder. In a separate shallow baking dish, put the beaten eggs.

Place one piece of tenderloin between two pieces of plastic wrap. Use a meat tenderizer, wooden mallet, or rolling pin to beat the tenderloin to ¼ inch thick. Repeat with the remaining tenderloin pieces.

Dip one piece of tenderloin into the flour mixture to coat and shake off any excess flour. Next, dip the lightly floured piece into the beaten egg and return it to the flour mixture. Slide the breaded tenderloin into the hot oil and fry for 4 to 6 minutes, turning, until it is golden brown. Remove to the prepared baking sheet to drain, and season immediately with more salt and pepper. Continue cooking the remaining pieces of tenderloin until all are fried. Serve each tenderloin atop a hamburger bun (the meat should be larger than the bun), and spread with Homemade Mayonnaise and Butt-Kickin' Ketchup. Fries are optional.

Butt-Kickin' Ketchup

yields 1 ½ cups

4 whole cloves

1 bay leaf

1 cinnamon stick

4 whole allspice berries

4 black peppercorns

2 pounds tomatoes, roughly chopped

1 ½ teaspoons kosher salt, or more to taste

½ cup cider vinegar, or more to taste

⅓ cup light brown sugar, or more to taste

1 sweet onion, roughly chopped

1 chipotle chile in adobo sauce, roughly chopped

1 clove garlic, smashed

Make a spice bundle of the cloves, bay leaf, cinnamon, allspice, and peppercorns, using a cheesecloth.

In a large saucepan over medium-high heat, combine the tomatoes, salt, vinegar, brown sugar, onion, chipotle, and garlic and add the spice bundle. Cook, stirring occasionally, for 20 minutes.

Remove the spice bundle and puree the sauce in a blender, covering the blender top with a towel, until the sauce is smooth. Strain the sauce through a fine-mesh sieve over the saucepan (why dirty more pans?) and return to low heat. Cook, stirring occasionally, for 1 to 1 ½ hours, until the ketchup begins to thicken. Season with more sugar, salt, or vinegar depending on your tastes. Let cool before serving (the ketchup will thicken as it cools). Butt-Kickin' Ketchup will keep, refrigerated, in a sealed jar, for up to 3 weeks.

Grilled Tenderloin and Romaine Salad

....

basil mayonnaise dressing ┊ salad ┊ serves 4

....

I don't know about you (well, I hope I know a little about you since you have this book in your hands),
but I am always looking for a full meal my husband can handle on the grill. This is it.
The perfect full grill meal. Just add a beverage.

2 heads romaine lettuce, halved lengthwise

2 tablespoons olive oil

Kosher salt

Freshly ground black pepper

1 pound Smithfield 🐷 pork tenderloin

1 lemon, halved and dipped in sugar

Basil Mayonnaise Dressing (recipe follows)

Freshly grated Parmesan cheese

Heat an outdoor grill, or indoor grill pan, to medium-high. Brush the lettuce with 1 tablespoon of the oil and sprinkle each half with salt and pepper. Set aside.

Use the remaining oil to coat the tenderloin. Sprinkle the tenderloin liberally with salt and pepper. Place the tenderloin on the hot grill and cook for 6 to 8 minutes per side. Remove from the heat and let rest for 10 minutes.

Put the lettuce halves flat side down on the hot grill and cook for 2 to 3 minutes, until a few grill marks begin to show on the leaves. The lettuce should still be crisp. Remove the lettuce from the grill and set aside.

Put the sugar-dipped lemon halves on the grill and cook for 3 minutes, until the sugar begins to caramelize. Remove and set aside.

Serve the salad family style on one platter or in individual servings. To assemble the salad, slice the tenderloin into thin slices. Arrange the lettuce halves on a platter or divide them among 4 plates and squeeze the fresh caramelized lemons over them. Top the salad with slices of tenderloin, drizzle with Basil Mayonnaise Dressing, and garnish with cheese.

Basil Mayonnaise Dressing

yields about 1 cup

1 cup Homemade Mayonnaise (page 80)

¼ cup fresh basil leaves

¼ cup freshly grated Parmesan cheese

Kosher salt

Freshly ground black pepper

Combine the mayonnaise, basil, and cheese in a food processor fitted with a metal blade and pulse until well combined. Salt and pepper to taste. (For a thinner dressing, stir in 1 tablespoon warm water.)

Jerk Roasted Tenderloin

banana chutney : entrée : serves 4 to 6

This dish was born of invention and necessity while on the island of Mayreau in the Grenadines, during one very long winter. The ingredients shouted out to me from hand-painted signs tacked on small homes along the narrow dirt back roads. "For Sale—Pig," "Banana," "Peppers," "Herbs and Rum." Rum was the appetizer, dessert, and floating message repository.

2 cloves garlic

2 tablespoons vegetable oil

2 tablespoons distilled white vinegar

1 tablespoon soy sauce

1 teaspoon ground allspice

Pinch of ground cinnamon

½ teaspoon freshly grated nutmeg

2 teaspoons dark brown sugar

2 teaspoons chopped fresh thyme

1 cup fresh parsley, chopped

1 bunch green onions, roughly chopped

1 large onion, quartered

½ cup freshly squeezed lime juice

Grated zest of 1 lime

2 teaspoons kosher salt

½ teaspoon freshly ground black pepper

1 Scotch bonnet pepper, seeded
(more if you prefer more heat)

1 (2-pound) pork tenderloin

Banana Chutney (recipe follows)

Put all the ingredients except the pork and chutney in a food processor. Pulse until the mixture forms a paste. Put the paste and the tenderloin in a 1-gallon zip-top bag and massage the paste into the meat to coat. Refrigerate overnight.

Preheat the oven to 350°F.

Remove the pork from the bag and discard any excess marinade. Transfer the paste-coated pork to a greased rimmed baking sheet. Roast for 18 to 20 minutes, until a thermometer inserted into the center of the meat registers 155°F (for medium doneness). Let rest for 10 minutes before slicing, and serve with Banana Chutney.

Banana Chutney

yields 3 cups

¼ cup golden raisins

2 tablespoons gold rum (I use Gosling's)

8 large bananas, mashed with your hands

1 large sweet onion, sliced

2 tablespoons minced fresh ginger

1 cup apple cider vinegar

1 cup packed light brown sugar

¼ Scotch bonnet pepper, seeded and minced

2 teaspoons kosher salt

Put the raisins and rum in a small bowl and let them soak overnight.

In a large saucepan over medium heat, stir together all the ingredients, along with the soaked raisins. Bring to a boil, stirring continuously. Lower the heat and simmer for 20 to 30 minutes, until the chutney sauce thickens. Serve warm. Any leftover chutney can be stored in a jar in the refrigerator for up to 2 weeks.

clockwise from top left:
Jerk Roasted Tenderloin,
Pork Chops and Applesauce (page 23),
Grilled Tenderloin and Romaine Salad (page 19),
Ribs St. Barthelemy (page 22)

BACK RIBS

Ribs St. Barthelemy

hot guava dipping sauce | entrée | serves 4

The island of St. Barts in the French West Indies inspired this sweet hot sauce. This lovely island is a place where the temperature, people, and sauces all compete for the title of "hottest."

2 (2-pound) racks
Smithfield **Baby Back Ribs**

Kosher salt

Freshly ground black pepper

Hot Guava Dipping Sauce (recipe follows)

Remove the membrane from the back of the rib racks (page 90). Liberally season the ribs with salt and pepper and let them sit at room temperature for 20 to 30 minutes.

Heat a grill to medium-high.

Wrap each rack of ribs individually in a double layer of heavy-duty aluminum foil. Place both rib packets on the grill and cook, covered, for 25 minutes. Turn the packets over and grill for an additional 20 minutes. The ribs will be done when the meat pulls away from the bone. To add a little crunch to the meat, unwrap the foil from the racks and place the ribs directly on the grill for 2 to 3 minutes per side. Remove the ribs from the heat and let them rest for 15 minutes before cutting them into individual servings. Serve warm or at room temperature with Hot Guava Dipping Sauce.

Hot Guava Dipping Sauce
yields 2 cups

½ habanero chile (less if you can't stand the heat)

8 ounces guava paste

1 cup freshly squeezed orange juice

Juice of 2 limes

2 tablespoons apple cider vinegar

1 cup fresh unsweetened coconut flakes

Kosher salt

Freshly ground black pepper

Put all the ingredients in a blender and process until smooth.

Guava paste is a mixture of guava pulp and sugar. It's a product of Brazil and Central America and is sold in 17 ½-ounce blocks that can be found in the ethnic food section of most grocery stores.

Pork Chops and Applesauce

entrée : serves 4

I would not be true to my youth if I did not reference Peter Brady here, but I prefer a better Brady bunch. One with Alice only using the best pasture-raised pig for her chops, Carol making her own applesauce, and Peter wearing J. Crew instead of that ridiculous red and white striped shirt.

4 (1-inch-thick) pork rib chops

1 teaspoon sea salt

½ teaspoon freshly ground black pepper

4 slices bacon, roughly chopped

Applesauce (recipe follows)

Season the pork chops with the salt and pepper and set aside.

Heat a large cast-iron skillet over medium-high heat, add the bacon, and cook until browned. Leave the cooked bacon in the pan and remove all but 2 tablespoons of the rendered bacon fat. Arrange the chops in the hot skillet with the bones pointing toward the center and sear the chops for 2 minutes on each side. Cover and lower the heat to low; cook the chops for an additional 5 to 8 minutes, until cooked to desired doneness. Serve them warm with Applesauce.

Applesauce

yields 3 cups

8 medium Fuji apples, peeled, cored, and sliced

½ cup apple cider

1 teaspoon freshly squeezed lemon juice

1 tablespoon unsalted butter

1 tablespoon brown sugar

½ teaspoon ground cinnamon

Pinch of ground cloves

¼ teaspoon ground allspice

Stir all the ingredients together in a Dutch oven over medium-low heat. Cover and cook for 20 to 30 minutes, until the apples are tender. Remove from the heat and mash the apples to your desired consistency. Serve warm.

Goat Stuffed Pig

pear pan gravy : entrée : serves 4 to 6

A goat stuffed inside a pig that even a monkey could prepare—it really is that simple. The creaminess of the goat cheese, the crunch of toasted pecans, and the tartness of the seasonal pears will make this pig one of your go-to favorites. The pear pan gravy will take it fresh from the farm and straight to heaven in one bite.

1 (2-pound) pork tenderloin

Kosher salt

Freshly ground black pepper

2 ripe pears, diced, plus 2 sliced firm pears

½ cup dried pears, chopped

2 cloves garlic, minced

4 ounces goat cheese, at room temperature

½ cup flat-leaf parsley, chopped

¼ cup pecans, toasted and chopped

1½ cups pork stock (page 154)

¼ cup pear brandy or apple brandy

1 cup apple cider

½ teaspoon minced fresh thyme

¼ cup heavy cream

2 tablespoons unsalted butter

Preheat the oven to 400°F.

To butterfly the tenderloin, use a sharp knife and make a lengthwise cut down the center of the tenderloin to within ½ inch of the bottom. Open the cut meat and lay it flat between two pieces of plastic wrap. Pound the meat until it is an even thickness. Remove the top sheet of plastic wrap and lightly salt and pepper the exposed side of the tenderloin.

In a small mixing bowl, stir together the diced ripe pears, dried pears, garlic, goat cheese, parsley, and pecans. Spread this mixture over the top of the tenderloin, leaving a clean 1-inch edge all around. Roll up the long side, removing the plastic wrap. Tie with butcher's twine every 2 inches to secure. Lightly salt and pepper.

Put the tenderloin in a shallow roasting pan along with the firm pears and ½ cup of the stock. Roast for 12 to 18 minutes, or until the internal temperature reaches 155°F. Remove from the roasting pan, cover loosely with foil, and let the tenderloin rest while preparing the gravy.

Meanwhile, use a slotted spoon to transfer the pears in the roasting pan to a bowl and keep them warm. Pour off any fat from the roasting pan, leaving only the meat juices on the bottom. Heat the pan over medium-high heat, add the brandy, and deglaze the pan for 1 minute, allowing the alcohol to burn off (be sure to scrape up all the brown bits on the bottom of the pan).

Whisk in the remaining stock, the cider, and thyme. Increase the heat to high and bring to a boil. Lower the heat and simmer, stirring occasionally, for 30 minutes, until the liquid is reduced by half. Stir in the cream and simmer for another 5 minutes. Salt and pepper to taste. Remove the pan from the heat and stir in the butter and pears.

Remove the twine from the tenderloin and slice it crosswise. Serve warm with the pear pan gravy.

Hot Brown Sugar–Rubbed Ribs

....

slow roasted : entrée : serves 4

....

A great cut of meat, six simple pantry ingredients, and three of the longest hours of
your life—waiting to taste these ribs.

2 (2-pound) racks Smithfield back ribs

¼ cup dark brown sugar

1 tablespoon ground cumin

2 tablespoons paprika

2 tablespoons chili powder

½ tablespoon kosher salt

1 tablespoon coarsely ground black pepper

Remove the membrane from the back of each rack of ribs (page 90). Discard the membrane and set the rib racks aside.

In a small mixing bowl, stir together all the remaining ingredients. Rub this mixture over the ribs. Put the ribs in a 2-gallon zip-top bag and refrigerate overnight.

Preheat the oven to 250°F.

Remove the ribs from the refrigerator and wrap the racks individually in a double thickness of heavy-duty aluminum foil. Put the wrapped racks on a baking sheet or in a shallow roasting pan. Bake for 2½ to 3 hours, until the meat pulls away from the bone. Carefully remove the wrapped ribs from the oven and let rest on a cutting board for 15 minutes with the aluminum foil intact, but opened at the top. Handle carefully— the rendered juices are very hot. Cut the racks into individual servings.

*clockwise from top left:
Country Smothered Pork Chops (page 28),
Hot Brown Sugar–Rubbed Ribs,
Grandma Lula Mae and Grandpa Russell Gibson on
their farm in Moberly, Missouri, October 1947,
Homely Rib Soup (page 29)*

Country Smothered Pork Chops

brown bacon gravy │ entrée │ serves 4

While preparing this dish you will need a cast-iron skillet and the ability to fend off a hungry family.

4 (1-inch-thick) pork loin chops

Kosher salt

Freshly ground black pepper

8 slices thick-cut bacon

Vegetable oil

1 cup plus 2 tablespoons all-purpose flour

1 small sweet onion, finely chopped

1½ cups beef stock

1 tablespoon chopped fresh sage

1 teaspoon Worcestershire sauce

4 cups hot cooked grits

Season the pork chops with salt and pepper and set aside.

Line a small baking sheet with paper towels. In a cast-iron skillet, fry the bacon until browned and crisp. Drain the bacon on the paper towels and crumble it when cooled.

Add enough oil to the bacon drippings in the skillet to fill it to ⅛ inch deep. Heat the fat until it is hot, but not smoking.

Put 1 cup of the flour in a shallow baking dish and dredge the seasoned chops in the flour until well coated. Shake off any excess flour and slide the chops into the hot oil. Fry the chops for 4 minutes per side, or until golden brown. Remove them from the skillet and keep them warm as you prepare the gravy.

Pour off all but 2 tablespoons of the fat from the skillet and place the skillet over medium heat. Add the onion and sauté for 5 minutes, or until golden. Stir in the remaining 2 tablespoons flour and cook for 4 minutes, until the onion is a deep brown color.

Slowly stir in the stock and cook, stirring constantly, for 6 to 8 minutes, until the sauce thickens and begins to boil. Reduce the heat to low and stir in the bacon, sage, and Worcestershire sauce. Salt and pepper to taste.

Return the cooked pork chops to the pan of gravy and simmer for 4 to 5 minutes, or until they are heated through. Serve over hot grits with a full ladle of bacon gravy.

Never walk away from your gravy. Stir it constantly.

Homely Rib Soup

paprika croutons : soup : serves 6

You don't wait until Friday night to ask a pretty girl out, but you can certainly have
this homely soup anytime you want her. And trust me: You'll want her.

4 tablespoons olive oil

2½ teaspoons kosher salt, plus more to taste

1 teaspoon smoked paprika

3 cups stale Italian bread, cut into large cubes

6 country style ribs

1 teaspoon coarsely ground black pepper,
plus more to taste

1 head garlic, peeled and smashed

8 cups pork stock (page 154) or chicken stock

½ cup grated Manchego cheese

Preheat the oven to 350°F. Grease a baking sheet and
set aside.

In a large mixing bowl, whisk together 2 tablespoons of
the oil, ½ teaspoon of the salt, and ½ teaspoon of the
paprika. Toss with the bread cubes. Spread out on the
prepared baking sheet and bake for 8 to 10 minutes,
until the bread is crisp and golden. Set aside.

Season the ribs with the remaining 2 teaspoons salt,
the pepper, and the remaining paprika. Heat the
remaining oil in a Dutch oven over medium-high heat.
Sear the ribs on all sides until browned. Remove them
to a dish and set aside. Using the same Dutch oven,
sauté the garlic for 4 minutes, or until golden. Return
the ribs to the pot, add the stock, and bring to a boil.
Lower the heat, add half of the croutons, and simmer
for 30 minutes. Salt and pepper to taste.

Ladle the soup into bowls, making sure there is one
rib per bowl. Top each bowl with croutons and cheese.
Serve hot.

Grilled Tenderloin and Fingerling Potato Salad

watercress, mustard vinaigrette | entrée | serves 4

1 pound pork tenderloin

7 tablespoons olive oil

Kosher salt

Freshly ground black pepper

1 pound fingerling potatoes

1 tablespoon Dijon mustard

2 tablespoons rice vinegar

1 clove garlic, minced

1 teaspoon honey

2 tablespoons capers, drained

2 cups watercress or arugula, stemmed

Rub the tenderloin with 1 tablespoon of the oil and liberally season it with salt and pepper. Let rest at room temperature for 20 to 30 minutes.

In a medium saucepan, put the potatoes and 1 tablespoon salt. Cover with cold water and bring to a boil. Lower the heat to a simmer and cook for 15 to 20 minutes, until the potatoes are tender. Drain and set aside.

Heat an outdoor grill or indoor grill pan to high. Grill the seasoned tenderloin for 8 minutes per side, turning only once. Remove the tenderloin from the grill and let rest for 5 minutes. Slice the meat and place the slices in a large mixing bowl. Set aside.

In a small mixing bowl, whisk together the mustard, vinegar, garlic, and honey. While whisking, gradually add the remaining 6 tablespoons oil in a slow, steady stream, until the vinaigrette sauce begins to thicken. Salt and pepper to taste.

Halve the potatoes and add them to the pork tenderloin slices. Pour the vinaigrette over, add the capers and watercress, toss to coat, and serve immediately.

how to

Prepare a Double Rack of Pork Ribs for a Crown Roast

entrée | serves 20

Two flat racks are lifted off the plate to become a regal crown roast in this step-by-step how-to.

2 racks of pork (10 to 12 ribs per rack), chilled

A sharp paring knife

2 bamboo skewers

Butcher's twine

1 Using a sharp paring knife, make vertical cuts along the outside and inside of each rib bone (as close to the rib as possible), extending to a depth of 3 inches down from the tips.

2 Make a horizontal cut between the ribs and remove all meat scraps. Refrigerate the scraps and save them to make sausage.

3 Using your knife and working patiently, scrape all the bits of meat, fat, and any stray membrane from every rib bone on both racks of pork.

4 Now you have two "Frenched" racks of pork.

5 Bend the rack into a circle with the rib bones facing up and the fatty side facing out.

6 Butt the ends of each rack together to complete the circle, and secure with two crisscrossed bamboo skewers.

7 Tie butcher's twine around the entire roast so that the twine rests just under the bone. Tie a second string around the roast 1 inch lower than the first.

8 The crown roast of ribs is done.

Freezing your rib racks for 20 minutes prior to trimming will help your knife go as close to the bone as needed for cutting, and will aid in the removal of the meat and fat from around each bone.

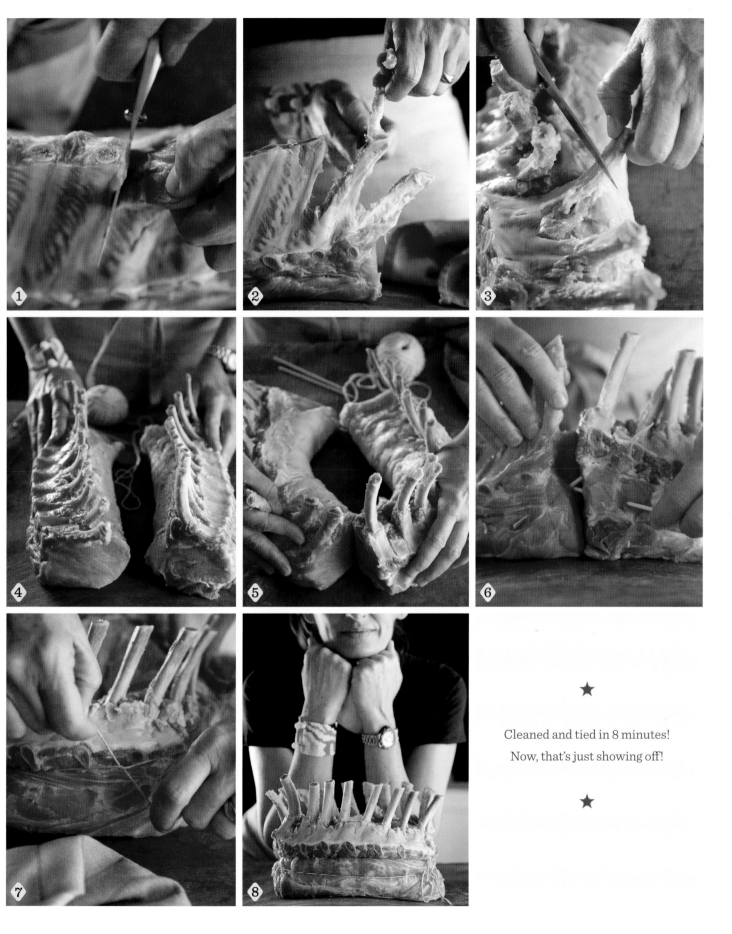

Cleaned and tied in 8 minutes!
Now, that's just showing off!

Lacquered Crown Roast

caramel orange sauce : entrée : serves 18

Tableside carving is mandatory, so concentrate your wardrobe around a great bracelet, ring, or cufflinks. No one will notice anything above the wrist, with all eyes on this spectacular crown roast.

1 (18- to 20-rib) pork crown roast (page 32), two racks of pork

Kosher salt

Freshly ground black pepper

1 cup sugar

2 tablespoons unsalted butter

3 tablespoons freshly squeezed orange juice

2 tablespoons freshly squeezed lime juice

1 tablespoon soy sauce

1 tablespoon fish sauce

Fresh bay leaves, for garnish

Set the roast on a heavy baking sheet. Liberally salt and pepper the roast and let it sit at room temperature for 30 minutes.

Preheat the oven to 350°F.

In a medium saucepan over medium-high heat, cook ½ cup of the sugar, without stirring, for 5 minutes, until the sugar starts to melt. Lower the heat to medium and swirl the pan. Continue to cook the sugar until it is completely melted. At any point during this process, if you need to release any sugar crystals that have formed, use a wet pastry brush to wash down the sides of the pan.

Add the remaining ½ cup sugar and cook, swirling, for 6 to 8 minutes, until a rich brown caramel forms. Turn off the heat and add ⅔ cup water. Raise the heat to high and cook, stirring continually, until the caramel is smooth. Remove from the heat and stir in the butter, orange juice, lime juice, soy sauce, and fish sauce.

Brush a thin layer of this "lacquer" over the crown roast and bake for 20 minutes per pound, or until a meat thermometer reads 160°F, basting the roast with the lacquer every 30 minutes. After you remove the roast from oven, baste it a final time with the lacquer. Let the crown roast rest for 15 minutes before slicing and serving, garnished with bay leaves.

Sweet and Sour Chops

entrée : serves 4

Sweet and sour ribs, sweet and sour roast, sweet and sour tenderloin—this sauce should never be limited to one cut of meat; it's perfect for all.

4 (8- to 10-ounce) pork rib chops, French trimmed

4 tablespoons olive oil, plus more for drizzling

Kosher salt

Freshly ground black pepper

½ cup balsamic vinegar

Pinch of cayenne pepper

Pinch of freshly grated nutmeg

3 tablespoons honey

6 tablespoons unsalted butter

1 tablespoon fresh thyme leaves, plus sprigs for garnish

Drizzle the pork chops with the 4 tablespoons oil and season them liberally with salt and pepper. Let the chops sit at room temperature for 20 to 30 minutes.

Heat a grill, or indoor grill pan, to medium-high.

In a small saucepan, stir together the vinegar, cayenne, nutmeg, and honey. Cook over medium heat until the mixture is reduced by half (about ¼ cup). Stir in the butter and thyme leaves.

Put the pork chops on the heated grill and cook, basting with the hot balsamic reduction, for 6 to 8 minutes per side, until browned and cooked through. Transfer to a serving platter and let the chops rest for 5 minutes before serving. Drizzle with the remaining balsamic reduction and oil. Garnish with thyme sprigs.

2

Boston Shoulder

blade Boston roast : blade steak : smoked shoulder roll : cubed steak

Boston shoulder

Probably the best barbecue you've ever eaten came from the Boston shoulder. This cut, which is also called Boston butt, comes from the upper shoulder of the pig running from the shoulder socket up to the spine. It consists of parts of the neck, shoulder blade, and the upper arm weave of muscles, fat, connective tissue, sinew, and bone. Usually an inexpensive cut and mostly lean, Boston shoulder has just enough fat marbling to keep the meat succulent during long, slow roasting or braising times. It is the cut of choice for pulled pork barbecue.

Cooking Methods: Best when slow roasted or braised, and for making ground pork and sausage.

Midnight Pork Tamales

It's not unusual for someone to receive a knock at the door in the middle of the night in a small town like Vandemere, North Carolina, where I once lived. It's a 287-person shrimping village, and you never know who might need something—a cup of milk, legal advice, help delivering a baby . . . So I wasn't too alarmed when I heard a knock on my door at midnight one summer evening. When I opened the door, there stood Pilar, one of the Mexican guys who worked in town as a crab picker, looking very serious. He spoke so fast that I couldn't make out what he was saying, but when I heard the word "tamale," I was all in. I had been begging Pilar for months to convince his wife I was good enough to be a student when she made her famous tamales and hoped upon hope this is what he was refering to. I threw on some clothes and followed Pilar to their cottage, just two blocks—and a world—away.

Stepping inside their door, I was overcome by the August heat and the heady smell of pork and chiles. I had a clear shot into the kitchen where Pilar's wife, Juanita, was laboring over a pan-filled stove—none too excited to see me. I tried to kill her with kindness in my very broken Spanish, but she barely looked at me. Clearly, she had work to do. Teaching me was apparently not on the list.

She wouldn't let me do anything. She moved around me, banging pots and sighing heavily. Then Pilar snapped at her. He must've told her that she needed to back off and let me do something because she slowed down just long enough to reveal this gorgeous pork shoulder she'd been cooking for God knows how long. I watched as she pureed the smoky chiles she had reconstituted in a fifty-year-old blender and poured them over the pork roast.

Without ever making eye contact, Juanita showed me how to assemble the tamale. She took a water-soaked corn husk and filled it with a thinly pressed disk of a masa-and-lard mixture. Then she added some of the seasoned pork, and one sliver each of a bean and potato from a can. She rolled it up and tied the ends with strips of husks. Then she held it up and said, in English, "See?" At first I thought she meant *sí* as in "yes," but from the smirk on her face I realized she actually meant, "See? This is how you do it, *gringa*."

Okay, got it. Game on, sister.

Six hours later, we each rolled our last tamale. The sun had come up some two hours before. I should have been weary and worn, but instead I was energized by what we'd accomplished. We probably averaged sixty tamales an hour—one per minute between the two of us. By the end, I figured that I had won Juanita over with my skills. She didn't thank me for my help, but she did send me home with some tamales. Baby steps.

A few days later, I bumped into Juanita at the post office. I was so excited to see her that I started rambling on about tamales, but she just looked down at the ground and walked out without saying a word. Okay, so maybe she wasn't willing to give me the respect I thought I had earned, but she had already given me something so much better: the secret of the Midnight Pork Tamale.

Midnight Pork Tamales (page 42)

Midnight Pork Tamales

entrée or appetizer : yields 20

30 corn husks

2 ounces dried Anaheim chiles

1 (2-pound) boneless Boston shoulder roast, trimmed and cut into 2-inch chunks

2 teaspoons ground cumin

4 cloves garlic, smashed

2 teaspoons kosher salt

4 cups pork stock (page 154) or chicken stock

4 cups masa harina

2 teaspoons baking powder

1 cup leaf lard (page 170) or vegetable shortening, melted, or corn oil

1 (14 ½-ounce) can green beans, drained

1 (15-ounce) can potatoes, drained, julienned into 40 pieces

Josh's Proportionate Margarita (recipe follows)

In a large mixing bowl, cover the corn husks with hot water. Use a plate to weigh the husks down and keep them submerged as they soak. Soak the husks, changing the water as it becomes cold, for 1 to 2 hours, until the husks become pliable.

Soak the chiles in a bowl of hot water to cover for 1 to 2 hours, until they are softened. In a blender, puree the reconstituted chiles with 2 tablespoons of the soaking water.

In a Dutch oven over medium-high heat, combine the pork, cumin, garlic, 1 teaspoon of the salt, 2 cups of the stock, and half of the chile puree. Bring to a boil, cover, and reduce the heat. Simmer for 2 hours, or until the meat is tender and can be pulled apart with a fork. Reserving 2 tablespoons, stir the remaining chile puree into the pulled pork and set aside.

Whisk together the masa harina, baking powder, and remaining 1 teaspoon salt in a large mixing bowl. Stir in the lard and the reserved chile puree. Gradually add the remaining stock until a spongy, thick dough—the consistency of cookie dough—forms.

To assemble the tamales, have the beans and potatoes ready. Wipe any excess water off the pliable husks. Tear 40 thin long strips from 10 of the husks to tie the tamales at each end once they are filled.

Working with one at a time, spread a ¼-inch-thick layer of dough over one of the whole corn husks, leaving a ½-inch space around the edges. Place 1 heaping tablespoon of the pork mixture in the center, along with 1 green bean and 2 pieces of potato. Roll the tamale up lengthwise and secure each end by tying with the corn husk strips. Repeat with the remaining husks, dough, and filling. (If you have leftover meat mixture, save it for a great pulled pork sandwich, or to enjoy with your morning eggs!)

To cook the tamales, use a large stockpot with a steamer insert (I use a large lobster pot); add water to a depth low enough that it will not touch the tamales when you place them in the steamer. Lay the tamales in the steamer and place a wet towel over them. Cover with the lid and steam for about 1 hour. You may need to add additional water during the cook time. To test for doneness, remove the husk from one tamale and unroll it. If the dough is sticking to the husk, it is not yet done. Steam the tamales for an additional 15 minutes. Serve them warm with Josh's Proportionate Margaritas.

Josh's Proportionate Margarita
yields 2 drinks

My husband, Joshua, is a wordsmith. A Paul-Smith-suit-wearing intellectual who sails yachts for a living and is oftentimes rudely stopped by his wife from waxing on about nothing and everything. This is his famous margarita. I had to sleep with him to get the recipe.

4 limes (or enough for 4 ounces of juice)

Kosher salt

3 cups ice

4 ounces silver tequila

1 ounce simple syrup

1 ounce Grand Marnier

Run the cut side of a lime around the rim of two 8-ounce glasses and dip each rim into salt to coat. Squeeze the limes and set the juice aside. Fill each glass with 1 cup ice. In a cocktail shaker, put the remaining ice and the tequila, lime juice, simple syrup, and Grand Marnier. Shake vigorously, and strain into the glasses.

Reconstituting chiles in cold water helps retain their original heat. Once reconstituted, if your chiles are too hot you can boil them to reduce some of their heat. Taste-test them, and if they are still too hot, rinse them, change the water, and boil them again.

Hot Pickled Pork Sandwiches

cool apple slaw · entrée · serves 8

If you have a slow cooker, set it up in the garage, because what this pickled pork recipe
lacks in skill to prepare, it makes up for in pungency while cooking.

**1 (2-pound) boneless blade
Boston pork shoulder roast**

1 (24-ounce) jar pickled jalapeño chiles,
with the pickling liquid

6 cloves garlic, whole

8 soft sandwich buns

Cool Apple Slaw (recipe follows)

In a slow cooker, cook the pork, chiles, and garlic on the low setting for 10 hours. When the meat is done, and while it is still hot, use a table knife or fork to gently break up the pork roast and mix all the ingredients well (everything will just fall apart). Serve on sandwich buns with Cool Apple Slaw.

Cool Apple Slaw

yields 4 to 5 cups

¼ cup Homemade Mayonnaise (page 80)

¼ cup sour cream

2 tablespoons cider vinegar

½ teaspoon kosher salt

½ teaspoon freshly ground black pepper

Grated zest and juice of 1 lemon

3 cups shredded red cabbage

2 Granny Smith apples, grated

2 medium carrots, finely grated

Don't have a slow cooker? A Dutch oven will also work great
with this recipe. Start on the stovetop and sear your pork roast
in 1 tablespoon of olive oil. Add the rest of the ingredients,
cover, and place the Dutch oven in a 250°F oven for 2 to 3
hours, or until the meat is fork tender.

Whisk together the mayonnaise, sour cream, vinegar, salt, pepper, lemon zest, and lemon juice in a large mixing bowl. Add the cabbage, apples, and carrots and toss to coat. Let the slaw stand, uncovered, at room temperature for 20 minutes, stirring occasionally. Refrigerate for 30 minutes and serve chilled.

clockwise from top left:
West African Pork Stew (page 46),
Hot Pickled Pork Sandwiches,
West Indian Pork Roti (page 49),
Cuban Pork Roast (page 47)

West African Pork Stew

sweet potato, peanut butter : entrée : serves 6

Kosher salt

Freshly ground black pepper

**1 (3-pound) boneless Boston blade pork roast,
cut into 1-inch pieces**

2 tablespoons vegetable oil

8 scallions, roughly chopped

3 tablespoons tomato paste

1½ tablespoons curry powder

1 tablespoon minced fresh ginger

¼ teaspoon red pepper flakes

1 large red bell pepper, seeded and chopped

2 pounds sweet potatoes, peeled and
cut into 2-inch pieces

4 cups pork stock (page 154) or chicken stock

⅓ cup natural peanut butter

¼ cup chopped fresh cilantro

⅓ cup chopped roasted unsalted peanuts

Liberally salt and pepper the pork.

Heat the oil in a Dutch oven over medium-high heat. Stir in the pork and cook for 6 to 8 minutes, or until browned on all sides. Stir in the scallions and cook for 2 minutes. Add the tomato paste, curry powder, ginger, red pepper flakes, bell pepper, sweet potatoes, and stock. Stir to combine, cover, and cook over low heat for 2 hours, or until the stew thickens. Stir in the peanut butter. Salt and pepper to taste.

Serve garnished with chopped cilantro and chopped peanuts.

Cuban Pork Roast

sweet cilantro rice | entrée | serves 8

This girl's own take on ropa vieja. There's only one caveat: The Miami Sound Machine must be playing during the preparation.

1 (4-pound) smoked Boston pork shoulder roll

Kosher salt

Freshly ground black pepper

2 tablespoons olive oil

2 cups white wine

2 medium sweet onions, thickly sliced

2 green bell peppers, seeded and cut into large pieces

2 jalapeño chiles, stems removed, halved

10 cloves garlic, smashed

1 (28-ounce) can whole tomatoes

2 tablespoons ground cumin

1 tablespoon ground coriander

2 tablespoons fresh oregano leaves

4 bay leaves

2 tablespoons Worcestershire sauce

4 tablespoons cider vinegar

Sweet Cilantro Rice (recipe follows)

Preheat the oven to 250°F.

Trim the pork shoulder of excess fat. Liberally season the pork shoulder with salt and pepper.

Heat the oil in a large Dutch oven over high heat. Sear the pork on all sides until it begins to brown. Remove the roast from the pot. Over medium-high heat, add 1 cup of the wine and deglaze the pot, scraping up all the brown bits of goodness from the bottom. Stir in the remaining ingredients. Return the pork to the pan and add enough water to cover. Cover the pot and cook in the oven for 6 to 8 hours, checking the liquid every 2 hours to make sure it just covers the pork, adding a little water as needed. Turn the pork roast over at least once during the cooking. When fully cooked, the meat will easily pull apart.

Remove and discard the bay leaves and shred the pork roast using two forks. Stir the shredded pork into the sauce. Serve with Sweet Cilantro Rice.

Sweet Cilantro Rice

yields 4 cups rice

2 cups long-grain white rice

2 cups coconut water (not coconut milk)

2 tablespoons unsalted butter

½ teaspoon kosher salt

4 tablespoons chopped fresh cilantro

Coconut water is the clear liquid inside young coconuts (not to be confused with coconut milk, which is actually the extract of the freshly grated meat of the coconut). As the coconut matures, the water is gradually replaced by the coconut meat and air. Coconut water is a great source of electrolytes, with less fat than whole milk and no cholesterol. You can usually find cans of both coconut milk and coconut water in the ethnic section of your grocery store.

Put the rice, 2 cups water, the coconut water, butter, and salt in a large, heavy saucepan and cover with a tight-fitting lid. Cook over medium-high heat until the water starts to bubble. Lower the heat to low and simmer, covered, for 20 minutes. Remove from the heat and let stand, covered, for an additional 10 minutes. Remove the lid, fluff the rice with a fork, and gently stir in the cilantro. Serve hot.

West Indian Pork Roti

There's a place in English Harbour, Antigua, I visited for the first time nearly twenty years ago. I found it by following the scent of fragrant curry down a dirt road. The source was a local restaurant called Grace Before Meals. Its proprietor is a wonderful Antiguan woman everyone calls "Auntie Grace." The restaurant is a little tin-roofed shack of a place, painted in pastel pinks and blues—the cutest thing you ever saw. Push-out windows propped open with sticks allow a welcoming harbor breeze into a dinning room so small that your knees touch your neighbor's. But if you're in a hurry (a relative term if you're on island time), you can order through the top half of a tiny Dutch door. Sure, it may take 20 minutes, but that's a small price to pay for a taste of heaven.

Everyone will tell you that Auntie Grace's specialty is roti. Roti originates in India (actually the word *roti* means "bread" in Sanskrit). But in the Caribbean, the dish takes on a whole different language. It's like a burrito of sorts. You have this incredible thin bread, and it's filled with a mouthwatering curried mixture of potatoes and meat of your choosing—chicken, conch, mutton, or goat. Now, I've had roti all through the Caribbean basin—the Leeward and Windward Islands, south to Trinidad, and all the way up—but no roti compares to Auntie Grace's.

Her mixture simmers all day on her six-burner stove. One bite and the meat just falls apart in your mouth. You barely have to chew. She also adds a special signature to her dish: a dollop of thick apricot jam. She adds it just before rolling the roti, and it transforms the dish into something magical. There's this savory curry flavor with sweet bursts of apricot jam mixed in. It's like roti-crack. Auntie Grace insists on a hibiscus drink to round out the meal. The first time I saw it, I thought it was a pitcher of red Kool-Aid, so I hesitated. But Auntie Grace can be pretty insistent when it comes to Caribbean cuisine, so she poured me a glass in spite of my protests. The raw, earthy hibiscus flavors juxtaposed with the curry and the sweetness of jam were simply amazing. Amazing Grace.

Luckily, because of my work in the yachting industry, I found myself in Antigua four or five times a year. Every time we docked, I went straight to Grace Before Meals to get the roti I'd been craving since my last visit. The first time I went there, I returned four times in one day. Eventually, Auntie Grace had to shuffle out from her kitchen in her flip-flops and baseball cap to see this American girl who was tossing back rotis like glasses of cold water. She took one look at me, smiled wide, and laughed.

"Well, she just a bitty thing!" she said.

Yeah, I thought, but not if I plan on staying in Antigua much longer.

West Indian Pork Roti

curried potatoes, apricot jam | entrée | serves 6

2 tablespoons unsalted butter

1 tablespoon vegetable oil

4 cloves garlic, minced

½ cup diced red onion

1 Scotch bonnet pepper, seeded and minced

2 tablespoons curry powder

1 teaspoon ground coriander

½ teaspoon kosher salt

1 pound smoked pork shoulder roll, cubed

4 russet potatoes, peeled and cubed

6 hot Roti (recipe follows)

6 tablespoons prepared apricot jam

Heat the butter and oil in a Dutch oven over medium heat. Stir in the garlic, onion, Scotch bonnet, curry powder, coriander, and salt. Sauté for 5 minutes, or until the onion is translucent. Add the pork and brown on all sides. Add the potatoes and 2 cups water and cook over medium heat for 20 to 25 minutes. Lower the heat and simmer for an additional 10 minutes. Remove the filling from the heat.

To assemble, fill the middle of each cooked roti with ½ cup of the filling. Top with 1 tablespoon of the jam. Fold the dough around the mixture to seal and serve immediately.

Roti

yields 12

4 cups all-purpose flour

1 teaspoon kosher salt

1 teaspoon baking powder

2 tablespoons vegetable oil

1 tablespoon unsalted butter, melted

Whisk together the flour, salt, and baking powder in a large mixing bowl. Slowly add the oil and 1 cup water, stirring continuously, then knead the mixture with your hands for 5 minutes. Form into a ball and let the dough rest for 15 minutes.

Divide the dough into 12 pieces of equal size. Roll 6 of the balls into 8-inch-diameter circles. Freeze the remaining balls in a zip-top bag for later use.

Heat a large flat cast-iron skillet or hoecake pan over high heat (for a larger cooking surface, try turning your cast-iron skillet over and using the flat bottom). Brush the skillet with butter and lower the heat to medium. Place one roti round in the pan and cook for 2 minutes, or until the dough starts to bubble. Flip the roti and cook the other side for another 1 to 2 minutes. Repeat with the remaining roti dough.

If your cooked roti becomes stiff while you are preparing the remaining rotis, simply put the fully cooked stack on a microwave-safe plate and cover tightly with plastic wrap. Microwave on high power for 25 seconds. Your roti should become perfectly pliable and ready for the filling.

how to

Make Green Grass Refrigerator Pickles | yields 2 quart jars

Grandma had a sunporch that was nearly falling off the southeast side of her old farmhouse. Each year, after the late-summer cucumber harvest, a rickety shelf running along the ceiling of the sunporch was lined with jars of the most unnaturally green sweet pickles a child could imagine. The same nuclear green pickles could be found in the refrigerator, for the grandkids to help themselves to. It was not unusual to be playing ball outside each summer and notice the players on both teams had green-stained fingertips. When I ate my first hot dog in Chicago, I finally came face to face with another relish as green as Grandma's. I was relieved to know my grandma wasn't the only crazy green pickle maker in the nation. Thank you, Vienna Beef. I'm forever grateful.

4 large cucumbers, skin left on

2 banana peppers

1 medium white onion

1 teaspoon kosher salt

2 cups sugar

1 cup cider vinegar

1 teaspoon celery seeds

4 drops green food coloring (optional)

1 Slice the cucumbers and peppers into thick slices, and the onion into thin slices.

2 Put the sliced vegetables in a large mixing bowl and sprinkle with the salt. Toss to coat and let rest for 1 hour at room temperature.

3 In a medium mixing bowl, whisk together the sugar, vinegar, celery seeds, and 1 cup water.

4 Add the green food coloring, if using, to the vinegar mixture. Whisk until the sugar is dissolved.

5 Transfer the cucumber mixture to 2 clean quart jars or other glass containers.

6 Pour the brine over the cucumber mixture, cover, and refrigerate for 2 days before eating.

7 Pickles are ready to eat. They are best when eaten within 2 weeks.

bottom right:
Ozark Mountain Barbecue Sandwich (page 52)

Pickles are best
when eaten within 2 weeks.

Try a few on my Ozark Mountain
Barbecue Sandwich
(page 52)

Ozark Mountain Barbecue Sandwiches

green grass refrigerator pickles | entrée | serves 12

Silver Dollar City is a place in Branson, Missouri, with hillbilly history. A Missourian's Mecca, if you will. My family made the pilgrimage by car when I was a young girl and still uncool enough to be giddy about the trip. My two older teenage sisters weren't of the same mindset. While their peers were back home planning extravagant lake parties and buying over-the-top twirly white dresses for debutante balls, they were stuck with their little sister learning from Ozark hill folk how to churn butter, barn dance, and turn wood into art. Of all the memories I have from that trip, a barbecue sandwich similar to this stands above all. As I took my first bite, I watched the rich juices run down the front of my shorts set and looked up to see both my sisters smiling for the first time since we left our driveway two days prior.

1 (3-pound) boneless Smithfield Boston shoulder roast, trimmed of excess fat and cut into 2-inch cubes

2 tablespoons all-purpose flour

2 teaspoons ground cumin

2 tablespoons chili powder

1 teaspoon dried oregano

1 teaspoon paprika

1 teaspoon kosher salt

1 teaspoon coarsely ground black pepper

4 tablespoons vegetable oil

2 medium sweet onions, finely diced

2 green bell peppers, seeded and finely diced

2 large carrots, peeled and finely diced

4 cloves garlic, minced

1 (28-ounce) can crushed tomatoes

½ cup dark brown sugar

½ cup prepared ketchup

2 tablespoons cider vinegar

2 cups pork stock (page 154) or beef stock

1 large bunch fresh parsley, chopped

12 sandwich buns, spread with butter and toasted on a griddle

Green Grass Refrigerator Pickles (page 50)

In a zip-top bag, combine the pork, flour, cumin, chili powder, oregano, paprika, salt, and black pepper and shake to coat.

In a large, heavy saucepan or Dutch oven, heat 2 tablespoons of the oil over medium heat. Add the spice-coated meat in batches and cook until the meat is browned on all sides. Remove the meat to a plate as it browns.

Add the remaining 2 tablespoons oil to the pan and stir in the onions, bell peppers, carrots, and garlic. Sauté, stirring often, for 5 minutes, or until the onions are soft. Be sure to scrape up all the brown bits from the bottom of the pan as you are stirring. Return the browned meat to the pan and add the tomatoes, brown sugar, ketchup, vinegar, and stock. Bring to a boil. Lower the heat, cover, and simmer gently for 2 hours. Uncover and continue to simmer for 1 additional hour. The sauce will begin to thicken.

Using two forks, pull the meat apart, shredding it. Stir in the parsley and serve the barbecue on the buns with Green Grass Refrigerator Pickles.

Pulled Pork Spring Rolls

island dipping sauce | entrée or appetizer | yields 20 rolls

4 cloves garlic

2 teaspoons Himalayan pink salt or kosher salt, plus more for sprinkling

1 pound boneless Boston blade pork roast

1 tablespoon vegetable oil

¼ cup minced sweet onion

1 cup shredded cabbage

½ leek (white part only), finely sliced

1 small carrot, finely grated

1 tablespoon oyster sauce

Freshly ground black pepper

2 quarts peanut oil for deep-frying

20 spring roll wrappers

Island Dipping Sauce (recipe follows)

Preheat the oven to 375°F.

Smash 2 of the garlic cloves with the salt to make a paste. Massage the paste onto the roast. Put the roast in a shallow roasting pan and cover it with aluminum foil. Bake for 2 hours, or until the meat pulls apart with a fork. When the roast has cooled, shred using a fork or your fingers and set aside.

Heat the vegetable oil in a large sauté pan over medium heat. Mince the remaining garlic cloves. Stir the onion, minced garlic, cabbage, leek, and carrot into the pan. Cook, stirring continually, for 5 minutes. Stir in the pork and oyster sauce. Add salt and pepper to taste. Remove from the heat and let cool.

Heat the oil in a deep-fryer or Dutch oven to 360°F. Have a very small bowl of water available. Line a baking sheet with paper towels and set aside.

Place 1 spring roll wrapper on a flat surface with a point facing you. Wet the opposite tip with water and put 1 heaping tablespoon of the pork mixture (be sure to drain off any excess liquid) in the middle. Fold in both sides and roll up. Repeat with the remaining wrappers and filling.

Slide the rolls into the hot oil and fry for 3 to 4 minutes, turning, until golden brown. Remove them and drain on the prepared baking sheet. Serve with the Island Dipping Sauce.

Island Dipping Sauce

yields 1½ to 2 cups

1 cup chopped fresh pineapple

Grated zest and juice of 1 lime

2 tablespoons chopped fresh cilantro

½ cup rice vinegar

3 tablespoons fish sauce

2 tablespoons brown sugar

1 teaspoon sriracha hot sauce, or more to taste

Combine all the ingredients, along with 2 tablespoons water, in a blender and blend until smooth.

Get ahead of the game! Make your party appetizers a day ahead. Pulled Pork Spring Rolls can be refrigerated for 24 hours before frying. Stack them on a lightly floured baking sheet and cover with plastic wrap. Fry them to order when your guests arrive. Island Dipping Sauce may be refrigerated for 1 week.

Bacon

slab bacon ⋮ sliced bacon ⋮ belly

bacon

Side pork, belly, or bacon—as it is referred to—is the fattiest part of the pig, resulting in unmatched flavor. Side pork is the fatty cut found under the loin and behind the ribs. It includes the skin, fat layer, and some thin muscle streaks. Because of its popularity, bacon is clearly the prom king of all cuts of pork. Thoughts of a properly braised pork belly sandwich for lunch will help you get up in the morning!

Cooking Methods: Nearly always cured, smoked, or both, to produce bacon.
Cuts of belly are best prepared by braising.

Pork Belly Gyros

For a stretch of four years, I was lucky enough to be a resident on the Greek island of Mykonos for a couple of months each year. I'd go to recharge my creative batteries, drink some ouzo, dive for sea urchin roe, and sleep. Standing on the edge of the cerulean blue Aegean Sea and overlooking the tan bodies of Grecian gods in Speedos, I knew I was exactly where I needed to be and where I needed to go next. Of course, as nourishing as all that introspection was for my soul, this girl needed to eat. And that's when I discovered the Mykonian gyro. I'd had gyros before. I bought one off a food cart in New York, ate a gut bomb from the county fair, and worse yet, ordered a gyro from some Midwestern chain where my server referred to it as a "gee-RO." Anywhere you live, someone's making some trashy gyro, but I'm here to tell you that there ain't no gyro like a gyro in Greece.

On Mykonos, I'd have to get on my dirt bike and ride ten minutes across the island from where I lived to get my hands on my beloved gyro. Then I'd have to wait in a long line with the rest of the gyro-philes, all itching for a fix. I couldn't say much in Greek—but I sure as hell could order a gyro just the way I wanted it. I wanted tomatoes, French fries, and tzatziki all wrapped inside wonderful just-baked flatbread that was oiled and warmed on the griddle. I didn't want any meat. I didn't want any onions. All I wanted was that warm flatbread and a few fillers to soak up that amazing sauce.

Over time, I made friends with the owner of the restaurant, Stavros, a man who also performed Greek dances for the tourists at night, and he let me in on a few secrets of the sauce. Most important, he explained, looking me deep in the eye for emphasis, you gotta let that stuff just marinate. Twenty-four hours. You can't make tzatziki sauce and eat it immediately because that garlic has got to marry in with the wonderful fresh cucumber, tangy vinegar, and the olive oil that smoothes it all out. And once you add the Greek yogurt, it's a perfect union.

I learned to perfect a tzatziki sauce of my own. Here I'm using this wonderful tzatziki recipe to make my pork gyros with silky pork belly. It's a simple recipe you'll find yourself making again and again. Grilling the marinated pork belly is absolutely amazing. A more perfect union.

Every place I've ever visited, I've come to associate with a dish. And the relationship between that food and the place it's from is so strong that I can't imagine ever experiencing the place without it. For me, Mykonos and gyros will forever go hand in hand. Together they represent summertime, beach, sand, and cute Greek boys—but that's another story.

Pork Belly Gyros (page 58)

Pork Belly Gyros

mykonian tzatziki sauce : entrée : serves 4

2 pounds pork belly, skin removed, cut into 1-inch strips

1 tablespoons dried Greek oregano

2 cloves garlic, minced

1 teaspoon freshly ground black pepper

4 Greek flatbreads or pita breads

2 tablespoons olive oil

1 tomato, cut into 8 wedges

½ red onion, very thinly sliced

1 cup Mykonian Tzatziki Sauce (recipe follows)

Put the pork belly strips in a zip-top bag along with the oregano, garlic, and pepper. Refrigerate for at least 2 hours, or overnight.

Heat a grill pan to medium-high and cook the pork belly for 4 minutes on each side, or until browned, for a total of 16 to 20 minutes cooking time. (Note: A lot of fat will be rendered; you may need to pour some off while cooking.) Cut the cooked meat into pieces.

Heat a large flat skillet over medium-high heat. Brush one side of each flatbread with oil and place the bread on the hot skillet until it is warmed through, but not toasted (the pita bread should still be very pliable).

To assemble, divide the cooked pork belly among the 4 warmed flatbreads. Top each with 2 wedges of tomato, some onion, and ¼ cup of the tzatziki sauce. Roll the flatbread up and individually wrap each gyro in a square of parchment paper. Serve immediately.

Mykonian Tzatziki Sauce

yields 1½ cups

1 cup plain Greek yogurt

2 cloves garlic, minced

½ cucumber, grated, well drained

2 tablespoons olive oil

1 tablespoon distilled white vinegar

Kosher salt

Freshly ground black pepper

Stir together the yogurt, garlic, cucumber, oil, and vinegar in a medium mixing bowl. Salt and pepper to taste.

For the best tzatziki sauce flavor, make it a day ahead and refrigerate. Let it come to room temperature before using, and stir it well before serving.

Rosemary Bacon Scones

sweet white chocolate · breakfast · serves 6

Without the rosemary, bacon, and white chocolate, this is a great go-to scone recipe for a lazy morning or afternoon tea. Adding the earthiness from the rosemary, saltiness from the bacon, and creamy sweetness from the white chocolate makes it a party anytime of the day.

2 cups all-purpose flour

1 tablespoon baking powder

½ teaspoon kosher salt

¼ cup leaf lard (page 170) or vegetable shortening, chilled

6 slices bacon, cooked crisp, drained, and finely diced

2 tablespoons chopped fresh rosemary

½ cup finely chopped white chocolate

1 cup milk

2 tablespoons heavy cream

1 tablespoon turbinado sugar or white sugar

Unsalted butter, softened

Preheat oven to 375°F. Line a baking sheet with parchment paper and set aside.

In a large mixing bowl, whisk together flour, baking powder and salt. Work in the chilled leaf lard with your fingers or two forks until mixture is crumbly. Stir in bacon, rosemary and white chocolate. Add the milk and stir just until the dough is sticky

Transfer the dough to a lightly floured surface and form into a large rectangle. Cut the rectangle into 6 long narrow triangles. Place the triangles on the parchment lined baking sheet about 1 inch apart.

Brush the tops of the triangles with heavy cream and sprinkle with turbinado sugar. Bake just until golden brown (approximately 12 to 15 minutes). Serve warm with butter.

Smokey and the Bacon Cheese Straws

appetizer · Yields 24 (10-inch) straws

¾ cup finely shredded cheddar cheese

¼ cup finely shredded smoked Gouda cheese

¼ teaspoon kosher salt

⅛ teaspoon chipotle chile powder

¾ cup plus 2 tablespoons all-purpose flour

¼ cup (½ stick) unsalted butter, chilled and diced

1 large egg, beaten

6 slices Smithfield naturally hickory smoked bacon, cooked crisp, drained, and finely diced

Preheat the oven to 400°F. Line two baking sheets with parchment paper and set aside.

In a large mixing bowl, combine the cheeses, salt, chipotle chile powder, and flour. Using a pastry cutter, two forks, or your fingers, work the butter into the flour mixture until pea-size pieces of dough form (add 1 to 2 teaspoons ice water at this point if the mixture is too dry). Stir in the egg and bacon and form a dough ball. Divide the dough in half; wrap one half in plastic and refrigerate.

Divide the unchilled dough portion into 12 pieces. On a lightly floured surface, use your hands to roll each piece into a 10-inch-long straw. Place the straws on a prepared baking sheet. Bake for 12 to 15 minutes, or until lightly browned and crisp. While the first baking sheet is in the oven, remove the second portion of dough from the refrigerator and roll and bake an additional 12 straws. Let cool before serving.

A few pulses in a food processor is a great way to finely dice your bacon. Bacon that is not diced finely enough will cause the cheese straws to break apart.

If the dough becomes too soft from the heat of your hands when rolling the straws, put it in the refrigerator for 10 minutes.

clockwise from top left:
Rosemary and Bacon Scones (page 59),
Smokey and the Bacon Cheese Straws,
Bacon Beignets (page 66),
Bacon and Cheese Puffers (page 63),
Savory Mushroom and Bacon Bread Pudding (page 67),
Porkovers (page 62)

Bakin' with Bacon

I ♥ bacon.

Cured bacon is my
vintage Chanel.

My last supper would
include bacon.

I am a baconista.

I've been intoxicated on
bacon-laced bourbon.

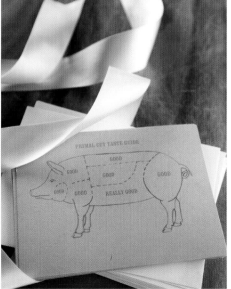

Porkovers

appetizer : yields 6

My mother-in-law and friend, Peggy, is the resident innkeeper of a fabulous old house in Annapolis, Maryland. During a Christmas dinner preparation not many years ago, Peggy was almost forced to look for a new job and accommodations when my popovers sounded the town's fire alarm. Always pushing the fat ratio, I went a little too far that year and used too much goose fat in the recipe. Luckily, it was only a stove and a few tiles that needed to be replaced. Now each Christmas dinner our son, Anthony, is in charge of the popovers. Each year they are better than the year before, but he still insists I am not allowed near the oven during their preparation. This recipe will clear my reputation once and for all.

4 slices bacon, cooked crisp, drained, and finely minced (rendered bacon grease reserved)

1 cup all-purpose flour

1 cup whole milk, at room temperature

2 tablespoons unsalted butter, at room temperature

½ teaspoon alderwood smoked salt or kosher salt

3 large eggs, at room temperature

Preheat the oven to 400°F. Using the reserved bacon grease, lightly grease the 6 holes of a popover pan and set it aside.

In the bowl of a food processor using a metal blade, combine the flour, milk, butter, salt, and eggs and process until the batter is smooth. Divide the batter equally among the popover holes. Sprinkle the tops of the popovers with the bacon and bake for 25 minutes (do not open the oven door!), or until the popovers puff up and are nicely browned. Lower the temperature to 350°F and continue baking for an additional 15 to 20 minutes. This added baking time will help set the center of the popovers. (There always is a little doughy center, no matter what you do—and this is my mother-in-law's favorite part.) Serve immediately! The popovers will only hold their puffiness for a few minutes.

After cooling, deflated Porkovers can be wrapped in plastic and placed in a zip-top bag to freeze. (Yes, I double wrap them!) To reheat, bake in a 350°F oven for 15 minutes. They make great soppy shovels for eating gravy and soup.

Bacon and Cheese Puffers

appetizer : yields 12 to 15

I learned this food processor shortcut for pâte à choux (pronounced pat-ah-shoe) from renowned French chef Jacques Pépin. My arm thanks him for the knowledge.

1 cup milk

¼ cup (½ stick) unsalted butter, cut into pieces

¼ teaspoon kosher salt

1 cup all-purpose flour

3 large eggs

Pinch of cayenne pepper

½ cup shredded Gruyère cheese

8 ounces bacon, cooked crisp, drained well, and finely chopped

1 tablespoon fleur de sel or kosher salt

Preheat the oven to 375°F. Line a baking sheet with parchment paper and set aside.

In a medium saucepan over medium-high heat, bring the milk, butter, and the ¼ teaspoon salt to a boil. When the butter has melted, remove from the heat and add the flour all at once. Using a wooden spoon, beat the mixture vigorously until it forms a ball. Return to medium heat and continue stirring for 1 minute, or until the mixture dries. Remove the mixture from the saucepan and spoon it into a food processor. Let cool for 5 minutes. After it has cooled slightly, process for a few seconds. Add the eggs and cayenne and process for another 15 seconds, or until it is well combined. Transfer the mixture to a mixing bowl and let cool for 10 minutes. Stir in the cheese and bacon until they are just incorporated.

Scoop out 1 heaping tablespoon of dough and push it off the spoon onto a prepared baking sheet with a second spoon (or use your finger). Repeat with the remaining dough, spacing the mounds 2 inches apart. Sprinkle the tops of the puffers with fleur de sel. Bake for 30 minutes, or until browned and crisp. Serve warm.

The abundance of bacon in these puffers makes them more dense than a basic pâte à choux.

Pumpkin Pie Pancakes

molasses bacon butter, green mango fool │ breakfast │ serves 4

I've never met a man who didn't love these pancakes. Heck, I've never met a man who didn't love any pancake, but these rank in the extra-special category. I pull this recipe out anytime I may need a little spousal redemption. Trust me, I'm no fool.

1½ cups all-purpose flour

1 teaspoon pumpkin pie spice

Pinch of ground ginger

½ teaspoon kosher salt

2 teaspoons baking powder

4 tablespoons sugar

2 large eggs

¼ cup (½ stick) butter, melted, plus more for the griddle

3¾ cup mashed cooked pumpkin

⅔ cup milk

1 teaspoon vanilla extract

Molasses Bacon Butter (recipe follows)

Green Mango Fool (recipe follows)

In a large mixing bowl, whisk together the flour, pumpkin pie spice, ginger, salt, and baking powder. In a separate medium-size mixing bowl, combine the sugar, eggs, butter, pumpkin, milk, and vanilla. Slowly pour the wet mixture into the dry mixture and whisk until just combined. Do not overmix.

Heat a griddle or skillet over medium-high heat and grease with butter. Pour ¼ cup batter for each pancake and cook until the pancakes bubble and the edges are dry. Flip the pancakes and cook the other side for 1 to 2 minutes. Transfer to a serving platter to keep warm. Repeat with the remaining batter. Serve warm with Molasses Bacon Butter and Green Mango Fool.

Green Mango Fool

yields 2 cups

2 green mangoes, peeled, pitted, and diced

⅓ cup sugar

1 cup cold heavy cream

In a medium saucepan, bring the mangoes, sugar, and ½ cup water to a boil, lower the heat, and simmer for 20 minutes, or until the mixture thickens. Remove the pan from the heat and let the mixture cool.

In the bowl of a stand mixer fitted with the whisk attachment, beat the cream until it forms stiff peaks. Fold the cream into the cooled mango mixture and serve.

Molasses Bacon Butter

yields ¾ cup

½ pound bacon, cooked crisp, drained, and roughly chopped

½ cup (1 stick) unsalted butter, at room temperature

1 tablespoon molasses

Put the bacon, butter, and molasses in a small mixing bowl and stir until just combined.

Bacon Beignets

lemon thyme curd · appetizer · yields 6 dozen

1 packet active dry yeast

½ cup granulated sugar

1 teaspoon kosher salt

2 large eggs, beaten

1 cup evaporated milk

7 cups all-purpose flour

2 teaspoons grated orange zest

¼ cup vegetable shortening

1 pound Smithfield bacon, cooked crisp, drained, and finely diced

Peanut oil for deep-frying

Confectioners' sugar

Lemon Thyme Curd (recipe follows)

In the bowl of a stand mixer fitted with the whisk attachment, put 1½ cups warm water (about 105°F) and sprinkle in the yeast. Stir to combine. Let the mixture to sit for 5 minutes, until the yeast begins to bloom.

Add the granulated sugar, salt, beaten eggs, and evaporated milk and whisk until well combined. Change the whisk attachment to a dough hook and add 4 cups of the flour and the orange zest. Beat until smooth. With the motor running, add the shortening, then gradually add the remaining flour. Add the bacon and beat until just combined. Cover the bowl with plastic wrap and chill the beignet dough in the refrigerator for at least 4 hours, or overnight.

Heat 4 inches of oil in a deep-fryer or Dutch oven to 360°F. Line a baking sheet with paper towels and set aside.

On a lightly floured surface, roll the dough out to ⅛ inch thick. Cut into long 1-inch-wide strips, then cut each strip into 2-inch lengths. Working in batches, deep-fry the beignets in the hot oil for 3 minutes per batch, or until they are lightly browned. Remove from the oil and drain on the prepared baking sheet. Sprinkle the beignets immediately with confectioners' sugar and serve hot with Lemon Thyme Curd.

Lemon Thyme Curd

yields 2 cups

3 large eggs

1 cup sugar

½ cup freshly squeezed lemon juice

1 tablespoon grated lemon zest

¼ cup (½ stick) unsalted butter, melted

2 teaspoons minced fresh thyme

Whisk the eggs and sugar in the top of a double boiler over simmering water until the mixture is light and fluffy. Stir in the lemon juice, zest, and butter. Continue cooking for 15 minutes until the mixture thickens. Remove from the heat and let the curd cool to room temperature. When cool, stir in the thyme. Can be stored in the refrigerator in a sealed container for 1 week.

For something different, substitute cinnamon sugar for the confectioners' sugar when you sprinkle the beignets. Beignet dough can be frozen after cutting. Place the cut pieces in a sealed container, and place waxed paper between the layers.

Savory Mushroom and Bacon Bread Pudding

warm sage butter : side : serves 6

2 tablespoons unsalted butter

1 pound thick-cut bacon

½ cup white wine

1½ pounds cremini mushrooms, roughly chopped

3 cloves garlic, minced

2 shallots, finely diced

1 tablespoon chopped fresh basil

1 tablespoon chopped fresh parsley

1 teaspoon rubbed dried sage

1 tablespoon chopped fresh thyme

Kosher salt

Freshly ground black pepper

5 large eggs

3 cups half-and-half

1 cup freshly grated Parmesan cheese

8 cups day-old challah bread, crusts on, torn into cubes

Warm Sage Butter (recipe follows)

Preheat the oven to 350°F. Grease an 8-inch square baking dish with the butter and set aside.

In a large sauté pan over medium-high heat, cook the bacon until it is crisp. Remove the bacon to a cutting board and chop. To the same skillet over medium-high heat, add the wine to deglaze the pan, scraping up all the brown bits as you stir. Stir in the mushrooms, garlic, shallots, basil, parsley, sage, and thyme. Sauté for 15 minutes, or until the mushrooms are tender and browned. Remove from the heat and stir in the bacon. Season with salt and pepper to taste.

In a large mixing bowl, whisk together the eggs, half-and-half, ¾ cup of the cheese, ½ teaspoon salt, and ½ teaspoon pepper. Add the bread cubes and toss to coat. Let the mixture stand for 15 minutes.

Stir in the mushroom mixture and transfer the pudding to the prepared baking dish. Sprinkle the remaining ¼ cup cheese over the top and bake for 40 to 60 minutes, until the pudding is browned and the center has puffed up. Drizzle with Warm Sage Butter before serving.

Warm Sage Butter

yields ¾ cup

¾ cup (1 ½ sticks) unsalted butter

6 fresh sage leaves, chopped

Melt the butter over low heat in a small saucepan. Add the sage and simmer for 3 minutes.

Savory Mushroom and Bacon Bread Pudding can also be made in individual ramekins. If you do so, reduce the baking time to 20 to 30 minutes.

how to

Wet-Cure Bacon | yields 1 pound bacon

1 (1½- to 2-pound) pork belly

1½ cups kosher salt

6 black peppercorns

6 bay leaves

1 onion, quartered

1 sprig fresh rosemary

3 cloves garlic, peeled and smashed

2 cups maple syrup

1 Remove the skin from the pork belly by slipping a sharp knife between the skin and the fat layer. I like to stay as close to the skin as possible because I like a bit more fat on my bacon. If you would like to cure a leaner bacon, trim as close to the meat as you want. Once you have the cut started, use one hand to pull the skin away from the belly as you run the knife under it.

2 In a large pot, combine the salt, peppercorns, bay leaves, onion, rosemary, and garlic. Pour in the maple syrup and 2 quarts water.

3 Place the pot over medium-high heat and, stirring, bring the brine mixture to a boil. Remove from the heat and let cool.

4 Once the brine has completely cooled (about 1 hour), strain it through a fine-mesh sieve.

5 Place the trimmed pork belly in a flat-bottomed dish and pour in enough of the strained brine to cover the belly by at least 1 inch. Leftover brine can be refrigerated for up to 30 days for curing more bacon.

6 Use a heavy plate or other weight to hold the belly down in the brine. Cover the dish and refrigerate in the coolest part of the refrigerator, with a constant temperature of 34°F to 36°F, for 4 days.

7 Remove the belly from the brine and pat dry. You now have bacon; it's that easy. At this point you may choose to smoke your bacon, but I prefer the unsmoked flavor. Slice if you like.

8 Wet-Cured Bacon can be kept refrigerated for 2 weeks and in the freezer for up to 3 months.

Salt, sugar, time, and constant temperature are the four key things you'll need when wet-curing bacon. There are many different schools of thought concerning the proper salt-to-sugar ratios. I am of the school that your brine, like your mate, should be sweet rather than salty.

The King's Belly Sandwich

| pork belly, peanut butter, banana butter | entrée | serves 4 |

When I was younger, I was obsessed with Elvis Presley. Okay, I still am. But back then, my imagination was so ripe I could picture myself on the brightly decorated sets of his formulaic movies, befriending costars like Shelly Fabares. Shelly would ask, "Libbie Marie"—I would, of course, change my name—"what did you and E do last night?" And I would fill her in on all the exotic fun a sheltered ten-year-old could dream up for a date with the King. Those were the innocent thoughts that filled a young heart. And these are the flavors, in honor of my first crush, My King, that satisfy an adult appetite.

1 (1-pound) pork belly

3 cloves garlic, chopped

5 fresh bay leaves, torn

Freshly ground black pepper

2 cups honey

2 cups soy sauce

¾ cup (1½ sticks) unsalted butter, softened

2 ripe bananas, mashed

¾ cup natural peanut butter

4 sandwich rolls

Prepare the pork belly by removing the skin if it is still intact (see step 1 of How To: Wet-Cure Bacon, page 68).

Heat a large cast-iron skillet over medium-high heat and sear the trimmed pork belly, beginning with the fat side down, for 5 minutes, turning, until it has browned on both sides and the fat begins to render. Remove from the pan and pour off all the rendered fat, reserving the fat for later use.

Preheat the oven to 225°F.

In a medium saucepan over medium heat, heat 1 tablespoon of the reserved rendered pork fat. Add the garlic and bay leaves and season generously with pepper. Cook, stirring often, for 3 minutes, until the smell becomes pungent. Stir in the honey, soy sauce, and ¼ cup of the butter. Cook, stirring continuously, until the honey dissolves. Return the pork belly, fat side up, to the skillet. Pour the garlic-honey mixture over it. Bring the liquid to a simmer and place the skillet in the oven. Bake, uncovered, for 2½ hours, basting occasionally with the pan liquids, until tender. Turn the pork belly once halfway through the baking time.

When the meat is tender, remove the belly from the skillet and let it rest for 5 minutes before slicing.

Meanwhile, in a medium mixing bowl, stir together the bananas and the remaining butter.

To assemble the sandwiches, slice the cooked belly into 4 equal pieces. Divide the peanut butter evenly among the sandwich roll bottoms and spread to cover. Top each sandwich bottom with a slice of pork belly and a generous helping of banana butter. Cover with the top bun and serve warm. The Elvis apron is optional.

Sliced Bacon

Thin Sliced
$\frac{1}{32}$ inch thick
28–32 slices per pound

Regular Sliced
$\frac{1}{16}$ inch thick
16–20 slices per pound

Thick Sliced
$\frac{1}{8}$ inch thick
10–14 slices per pound

Fiery Roasted Tomato Soup

soup : serves 4

Once you make tomato soup this way, you'll never go back to another. One roasting pan filled with everything you love except your lover. Roast. Puree. Eat.

6 slices bacon

2 tablespoons olive oil

8 medium tomatoes, left whole

2 shallots, diced

2 cloves garlic, smashed

3 carrots, peeled and chopped

1 small sweet onion, chopped

1 jalapeño chile, stem removed, halved

1 teaspoon kosher salt

¼ teaspoon freshly ground black pepper

Preheat the oven to 425°F.

In a large roasting pan, toss together all the ingredients. Roast for 40 minutes, or until a little color starts to show and the vegetables begin to soften. Halfway through the cooking time, stir the ingredients and remove the cooked bacon. Chop the bacon and set aside for garnish. Working in batches, transfer the contents of the roasting pan to a blender and puree. Serve warm, garnished with the bacon.

clockwise from top right:
Fiery Roasted Tomato Soup,
Crispy Thai Pork Belly (page 75),
Pan-Fried Brussels Sprout Leaves (page 74)

This soup is so thick you can use it as a quick roasted tomato red sauce on your favorite pasta. If you want to thin it down a bit, just add a little of your pasta water. Garnish with chopped fresh basil and shaved Parmesan cheese.

Pan-Fried Brussels Sprout Leaves

crispy pancetta : side : serves 4

Trust me on this, part of cooking is about tactics.

Everyone who tastes this dish raves about its flavor and simplicity. Unfortunately, the time necessary to separate the leaves is time I never seem to have. What do I do, then? I save this dish for a dinner party, that's what I do! Since this super side must be cooked only moments before you sit down to dinner, I like to give the tedious job of separating the leaves to one of "my eager to help" and way too early guests. Tactics, baby, tactics.

8 ounces pancetta, chopped

1 tablespoon olive oil

2 cloves garlic, minced

2 shallots, thinly sliced

1 pound Brussels sprouts, ends removed, leaves individually separated

½ teaspoon red pepper flakes

¼ teaspoon freshly ground black pepper

¼ cup freshly grated Parmesan cheese

In a large skillet over medium heat, cook the pancetta for 5 to 7 minutes, until crisp. Using a slotted spoon, remove the pancetta to a paper towel–lined plate to drain. Sauté the oil, garlic, shallots, Brussels sprouts leaves, red pepper flakes, and pepper for 5 minutes, or until the Brussels sprout leaves are beginning to brown and turn crisp. Return the pancetta to the pan and stir. Sprinkle with the cheese and serve immediately.

Crispy Thai Pork Belly

sweet lime sauce : entrée or appetizer : serves 4

The Thai call it moo krawp. I call it the best parts of the pig. Fat, skin, and meat.

1 pound pork belly (4 to 5 inches thick)

4 tablespoons distilled white vinegar

¼ cup kosher salt, plus more for sprinkling

4 cups peanut oil

Sweet Lime Sauce (recipe follows)

Put the pork belly in a large stockpot and cover with water. Add 3 tablespoons of the vinegar and 1 teaspoon of the salt and bring to a boil. Boil for 45 minutes, or until the skin is tender. Remove the pork belly from the pot and let rest until cool enough to handle. Using a sharp knife, score the skin of the pork belly ¼ inch deep, using a 1-inch crisscross pattern (scoring will give the belly more places to crisp up when it is fried).

Put the pork belly in a shallow baking dish, skin side up, and brush the remaining vinegar over the entire surface. Sprinkle with the remainder of the ¼ cup salt. Refrigerate, uncovered, for at least 4 hours, or overnight. When you are ready to cook, remove the belly from the refrigerator and pat it dry.

In a deep-fryer, heavy wok, or Dutch oven, heat the oil (enough oil to cover the belly by 1 inch) to 325°F. Line a plate with paper towels and set aside.

Gently slide the belly into the hot oil and give it a little nudge with tongs to make sure it does not stick to the bottom of the pan. If oil splatters (most likely it will), cover the pan with a loose lid or a piece of aluminum foil. Cook for 6 minutes, or until the belly is golden brown and crisp. Drain the belly on the prepared plate and sprinkle it with salt. Slice and serve hot with Sweet Lime Sauce for dipping.

Sweet Lime Sauce

yields about ⅓ cup

2 tablespoons freshly squeezed lime juice

2 tablespoons fish sauce

2 tablespoons brown sugar

1 tablespoon soy sauce

1 tablespoon chopped fresh cilantro, plus more for garnish

1 Thai bird chile, finely chopped (or more if you like extra heat)

In a small mixing bowl, whisk together all the ingredients until the sugar dissolves. Garnish with cilantro. Serve.

Southern Peanut Soup

soup | serves 6

This soup is a true Southern belle—full of charm, a little bit nutty, and always crosses her legs at the ankle. Well, maybe not the ankle thing, but you get my drift.

6 slices Smithfield bacon

1 medium sweet onion, finely chopped

6 celery hearts with leaves, finely chopped

4 cups good-quality chicken stock

2 tablespoons all-purpose flour

1 cup heavy cream

1 cup natural peanut butter

1 pint half-and-half

Kosher salt

Freshly ground black pepper

Chopped roasted peanuts

Line a baking sheet with paper towels and set aside.

In a large saucepan over medium heat, cook the bacon until crisp, drain on paper towels, and chop. Pour off all but 2 tablespoons of the bacon drippings from the pan. To the pan, add the onion and celery and sauté over medium heat for 1 minute. Cover the pan and lower the heat to low. Cook for 15 minutes, until the vegetables are soft and translucent.

In a medium saucepan over medium-high heat, bring the stock to a low boil.

Stir the flour into the onion mixture and cook, stirring often, until the mixture is a golden color with a nutty aroma. Add the hot stock to the flour mixture in a slow, steady stream, whisking constantly. Whisk in the cream and cook, whisking continually, for 5 minutes, or until mixture is heated through. Whisk in the peanut butter until it is fully incorporated. Cook for 6 to 8 minutes. Whisk in the half-and-half and cook for 5 minutes. Salt and pepper to taste. Strain the soup through a fine-mesh sieve and ladle it into bowls while it is hot. Garnish with the bacon and peanuts.

Try Southern Peanut Soup as a soup-shooter appetizer at your next party . . . themed, of course—this is a Southern belle.

Dinnertime Donuts

moon gate bacon jam | appetizer | yields 24 donuts

Eighteen years ago, on my first visit, I fell in love in Bermuda—and with Bermuda.

The Island of Bermuda is a place I've had the great fortune to travel to often—arriving by boat when I worked as a cook aboard sailing yachts, and now arriving by plane, just a short flight from my home in Savannah. I've eaten the best pork in my life on this small island (from descendants of wild hogs that are fed on the sweet native grasses of the island), and I've aggressively sampled the butterscotch and vanilla-flavored Goslings Black Seal rum aged there. This tempestuous rum has left me washed up on a pink sandy beach more than once, and earned its rightful place in my current liquor cabinet inside the only crystal decanter I own. I've walked past and through the garden moon gates found throughout the island . . . hoping to be blessed with the good luck that, as the legend has it, is given to all who walk through. It's funny how a dish sometimes embodies a physical place in our lives. These Dinnertime Donuts, with their moon gate curve and Bermudian rum–laced bacon jam, are a tribute to an island that means so very much to me.

¾ cup warm milk

¼ cup sugar

1 packet active dry yeast

2½ cups all-purpose flour, plus extra for dusting

¼ teaspoons kosher salt

2 tablespoons unsalted butter, at room temperature

2 large egg yolks

Peanut oil or vegetable oil for deep-frying

Moon Gate Bacon Jam (recipe follows)

In the bowl of a stand mixer fitted with the dough hook, combine the milk, sugar, and yeast. Let the mixture rest for 10 minutes, until the yeast starts to foam.

In a medium mixing bowl, whisk together the flour and salt. Add the flour mixture, butter, and egg yolks to the yeast mixture and mix on medium speed for 3 to 5 minutes, until the dough comes together and forms a ball. Cover the bowl and let the dough rise in a warm place for 1 hour.

Grease a large baking sheet and set aside.

Transfer the dough to a lightly floured work surface and roll out to ½ inch thick. Using a 2- to 3-inch donut cutter (you can also use a drinking glass or biscuit cutter to cut out your donut rounds, and a plastic bottle cap to cut out the holes), cut out the donuts and transfer them and their holes to the prepared baking sheet, spacing them 1 inch apart. Spray the tops of the donuts and the holes with nonstick cooking spray and cover loosely with plastic wrap. Let the donuts stand in a warm place for 30 to 45 minutes, until they have almost doubled in size.

In a deep-fryer or Dutch oven, heat 4 inches of oil to 350°F. Line a baking sheet with paper towels and set aside.

Working in batches, fry the donuts and donut holes for 1 minute per side, until they are a light golden brown color. Transfer to the prepared baking sheet. Serve the donuts warm with the Moon Gate Bacon Jam.

Moon Gate Bacon Jam

yields ½ cup

6 ounces sliced bacon

½ cup chopped shallots

About 2 tablespoons Bermuda Black Seal rum

About 3 tablespoons dark brown sugar

3 cups pork stock (page 154)

Pinch of cayenne pepper

Kosher salt

Freshly ground black pepper

2 tablespoons unsalted butter

Preheat the oven to 500°F.

In a medium-sized, heavy, oven-safe sauté pan, cook the bacon in the oven for 12 to 15 minutes, until it is crisp and the fat has rendered. Remove the cooked bacon from the pan and reserve it for another use, leaving the rendered fat in the pan. Add the shallots to the rendered fat, return the pan to the oven, and cook the shallots for 10 minutes, or until they turn dark brown. Remove the pan from the oven and stir in enough rum and brown sugar to barely coat the shallots. Stir in 1 cup of the stock and return the pan to the oven to simmer for 15 to 20 minutes, until the mixture begins to thicken. Working quickly, add 1 cup of the remaining stock to the jam and continue to simmer in the oven for 40 minutes to thicken. Remove from the oven and stir in the cayenne and the remaining stock. Salt and pepper to taste. Carefully pour the mixture into a blender and puree until smooth. Pour the pureed mixture back into the hot pan and return the pan to the oven for 30 minutes, stirring frequently, until the jam turns a dark, earthy color. Remove from the oven and stir in the butter. Let the jam cool slightly. Use sparingly. Moon Gate Bacon Jam is very rich and flavorful—a little goes a very long way.

Dinnertime Donuts are meant to be a savory dish, but if served with a sprinkling of powdered sugar or simply dipped in chocolate frosting, they make the breakfast table smile. When serving the donuts as a savory, remember the Moon Gate Bacon Jam is a labor of love and is not to be overused. One donut requires a mere "toe in the water" using this jam.

World's Best BLT

grilled green tomatoes, homemade mayo | entrée | serves 4

If you're traveling to remote places, a red tomato is sometimes hard to find. Surprisingly, I've found that a green tomato isn't. This revelation still upsets my sensibilities, but I have learned to embrace it. When I worked for yachting clients around the world, I made my BLTs using green tomatoes. Each time I made them, I'd hear the same thing: "Libbie, this is the best BLT I've ever had." Thus its name is earned.

2 firm green tomatoes, each cut into 4 thick slices

2 tablespoons vegetable oil

Kosher salt

Freshly ground black pepper

8 slices sunflower bread

2 cups green-leaf lettuce, cut into thin ribbons

2 teaspoons freshly squeezed lemon juice

1 cup Homemade Mayonnaise (recipe follows)

12 slices bacon, cooked crisp and drained

Heat a grill or indoor grill pan to high.

Brush the tomato slices with 1 tablespoon of the oil and sprinkle them with salt and pepper. Place the tomatoes on the hot grill and cook for 3 to 4 minutes per side, until brown marks appear. Set aside. Grill the bread slices and set aside.

Put the lettuce in a medium mixing bowl. Drizzle with the remaining oil and the lemon juice, and salt and pepper to taste. Using tongs, toss the greens to coat.

Spread a thick layer of mayonnaise on one side of all 8 slices of bread. Top 4 slices of bread with 3 slices of bacon each, 2 grilled green tomato slices, and one-quarter of the dressed greens. Place the remaining 4 bread slices (mayonnaise side down) on top of each sandwich.

Homemade Mayonnaise

yields ¾ cup

2 large egg yolks

1 teaspoon distilled white vinegar

2 teaspoons freshly squeezed lemon juice

½ teaspoon dry mustard powder

¼ teaspoon cayenne pepper

½ teaspoon kosher salt

¾ cup vegetable oil

Combine the egg yolks, vinegar, lemon juice, mustard powder, cayenne, and salt in a medium mixing bowl. Whisk for 1 minute, or until the mixture is well combined and bright yellow in color. Add ¼ cup of the oil a few drops at a time, whisking constantly. It's important not to rush this step, because the oil must be fully incorporated after each addition. This step will take about 5 minutes. Continuing to whisk for 8 to 10 minutes more, gradually add the remaining ½ cup oil in a slow, steady stream until the mayonnaise begins to thicken and lighten in color. The mayonnaise will keep for 2 days, covered and refrigerated.

Spare Ribs

spare ribs | salt pork

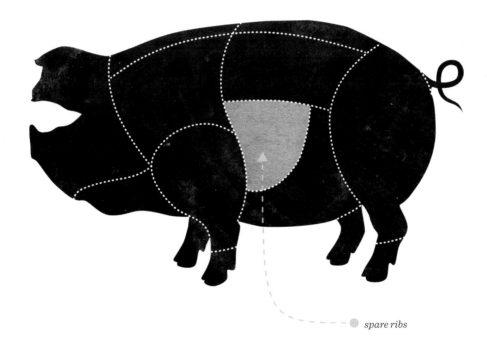

spare ribs

Back-road rib joints all across the South are known for their spare ribs bathed in a special house sauce and served on a slice of white bread. Spare ribs or "spares," as they are sometimes called, are cut from the belly side of the ribs where they join the breastbone. The bones are straighter and flatter than back ribs, and the meat has more of the fat marbling. Spare ribs are typically less expensive than back ribs because they have more bone than meat. The meat used to make salt pork is often cut from this same area of the belly. Although salt pork resembles bacon, it is considerably saltier. It is a great flavor enhancer to vegetables cooked in water.

Cooking Methods: Best cooked very slowly over low temperatures, usually by braising or roasting. Salt pork is generally blanched or rendered before use.

South Cackalacky Spare Ribs

mustard barbecue sauce : entrée : serves 4

Growing up in Missouri, I didn't know there was anything but St. Louis or Kansas City barbecue sauce. Then I began to travel, and aside from their state college teams, the only other thing Americans of different regions seemed to be exceptionally passionate about was their barbecue sauce. If you live in North Carolina, chances are you are a Tar-Heel and vinegar-based-sauce fan (no one cares about Duke fans). Texas, well that's all about A&M or the Longhorns. Though divided in rivalry, both sides unite when they reach for the same sweet spicy ketchup-based sauce for their brisket. Then there's the folks from South Carolina. If you ever meet anyone from there, you'll know it. They're usually wearing some sort of Gamecocks or Clemson schwag (whether they are an alumni of either institution or not); they actually use the phrase "South Cackalacky" when they get liquored up; and they will always reach for the yellow barbecue sauce on the table. This sauce they'll be fighting for.

4 pounds pork spare ribs

2 teaspoons kosher salt

2 teaspoons coarsely ground black pepper

1 teaspoon ground cumin

2 teaspoons paprika

1 tablespoon brown sugar

1 teaspoon cayenne pepper

Mustard Barbecue Sauce (recipe follows)

Trim any large areas of excess fat and the membrane from the back of the ribs (page 90).

In a small mixing bowl, whisk together all the remaining ingredients, except the sauce. Rub this mixture into the ribs on both sides. Wrap the ribs in plastic wrap and refrigerate for 2 hours before cooking.

Preheat one side of your grill to medium-high.

Grill the meat, rib side down, on the side of the grill, not over a direct flame. Use the indirect heat to cook the ribs for 2 hours, until the meat begins to pull away from the bones. Brush the ribs with mustard sauce 5 minutes before removing them from the grill. Serve the ribs with the remaining sauce on the side.

Mustard Barbecue Sauce
yields 2 cups

1 cup prepared yellow mustard

$\frac{1}{4}$ cup molasses

$\frac{1}{4}$ cup honey

2 tablespoons brown sugar

$\frac{1}{4}$ cup cider vinegar

1 tablespoon vegetable oil

$\frac{1}{4}$ teaspoon ground oregano

$\frac{1}{4}$ teaspoon ground thyme

$\frac{1}{4}$ teaspoon freshly ground black pepper

$\frac{1}{4}$ teaspoon cayenne pepper

Put all the ingredients in a 1-quart jar, cover, and shake vigorously until well combined.

Don't let anyone go hungry. Since spare ribs are mostly bones, always allow 1 pound (uncooked weight) per person.

Citrus Sugar-Rubbed Ribs

mediterranean spice | entrée | serves 4

6 tablespoons raw cane sugar or white sugar

2 teaspoons kosher salt

½ teaspoon white pepper

1 teaspoon dried dill

½ teaspoon dried mint

Pinch of dried oregano

Grated zest of 2 lemons

Grated zest of 2 oranges

2 (2-pound) slabs spare ribs

In a small mixing bowl, whisk together all the ingredients except the ribs. Set aside.

Trim any large areas of excess fat and the membrane from the back of the ribs (page 90).

Rub the citrus-sugar mixture over the ribs and massage it into the meat. Place the racks, separately, in two 2-gallon zip-top bags. Seal and refrigerate overnight.

Preheat the oven to 250°F.

Remove the ribs from the bags and wrap each rack separately in a double layer of heavy-duty aluminum foil. Put the rib packets in a shallow roasting pan and bake for 2½ to 3 hours, until the meat pulls away from the bones and is fork tender. Turn the ribs halfway through the cooking process. Remove from the oven, open the foil at the top without removing the ribs, and let the ribs rest on a cutting board for 15 minutes. Remove the foil completely and cut the ribs into individual portions to serve.

Salt Pork Cabbage and Leeks

side : serves 8

Salt pork adds the flavor to this sprightly side dish, but using a slice of last week's country ham would taste just as wonderful.

8 ounces salt pork, rinsed, dried, and diced

1 large sweet onion, chopped

2 leeks (white parts only), rinsed and thinly sliced

1 tablespoon Texas Pete hot sauce, or your favorite

2 small heads cabbage, cored and sliced

Freshly ground black pepper

In a large Dutch oven over medium heat, cook the salt pork until it just begins to brown. Add the onion and leeks and cook for 5 minutes, until the onion is translucent. Stir in the hot sauce and cabbage. Cook, stirring occasionally, for 8 to 10 minutes, until the cabbage is just wilted but still has a bit of firmness. Pepper to taste.

Use this recipe as a great filler for spring rolls, or mix it in with a little fresh pasta for dinner on the fly—and the cheap.

Baked White Beans

sweet spiced salt pork · side · serves 6 to 8

Who said baked beans had to be baked and couldn't be white?

1 pound dried navy beans

2 tablespoons olive oil

¼ pound salt pork or bacon, rinsed thoroughly and cut into ½-inch pieces

1 sweet onion, roughly chopped

2 cloves garlic, minced

1 teaspoon dried oregano

½ teaspoon ground cumin

¼ cup honey

¼ cup molasses

2 tablespoons brown sugar

2 tablespoons stone-ground mustard

Rinse the beans well and soak them overnight in enough water to cover. In the morning, drain the beans and rinse again.

In a Dutch oven, heat the oil over medium heat. Stir in the salt pork, onion, garlic, oregano, and cumin and cook for 2 minutes. Stir in the beans and add enough fresh water to cover them. Stir in the remaining ingredients and bring the mixture to a low boil. Lower the heat to low, stir the beans, and cover with a tight-fitting lid. Cook over low heat for 2 hours, stirring occasionally, until the beans are tender.

Baked White Beans can also be prepared in a slow cooker. Put the beans in the slow cooker, cover with fresh water, and stir in the remaining ingredients. Cook on the low setting for 12 hours, stirring occasionally.

clockwise from top left:
Baked White Beans,
me at the St. Charles County Fair Pig Scramble (1973),
Salt Pork Cabbage and Leeks (page 87),
my big sister Robbie at the St. Charles County Fair
Pig Scramble (1973)

how to

Remove the Pork Rib Membrane

There are two schools of thought about removing the membrane (peritoneum) from the bone side of a rack of ribs before cooking. A smattering of (crazy) people believe leaving the membrane on does not effect the taste. I am of the (sound) mindset that it must go. I find my ribs much more flavorful and tender when the rub, marinade and smoke from the fire are able to penetrate both sides of the rack. Removing the membrane is really quite simple. Like pulling off an old bumper sticker, the trick is finding a good edge.

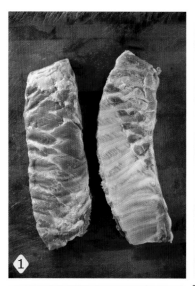

1 Turn the rack so the rib side (concave side) is facing up.

2 Slip a sharp knife between the membrane and the meat on one edge of the rack and lift up enough to get a good grip on the membrane. At this point, if the membrane is thick, you can work your fingers under it to loosen it a bit, in order to get a good grip.

3 Hold the rack down with one hand, and with your other hand firmly gripping the membrane, pull the membrane away from the ribs completely. If the membrane tears, don't worry. Use your knife to lift up another corner and repeat the process.

4 Trim excess fat from both sides of the rib rack. Your ribs are now ready to season and cook.

Welcome Home Oven-Barbecued Spare Ribs

pineapple chili sauce ⋮ entrée ⋮ serves 4

If you've ever driven south from Montgomery toward Mobile and gotten lost on County Road 10, you may have happened upon Pine Apple, Alabama, population 145. This hamlet is famous for having one of the longest deer seasons in the country and has two places on the National Register of Historic Places. The pineapple symbol of hospitality seems to be everywhere you look. Pineapples carved on doors, painted on mailboxes, and spelled out on signs. I happened upon the town one blisteringly hot Alabama Sunday afternoon while a historic tour was in progress. Pineapple signs marked each site along the tour, and handicrafts sold at all the tour stops were emblazoned with the hospitable fruit. The only thing this heathen couldn't get in Pine Apple, Alabama, that Sunday afternoon was a piña colada.

2 (2-pound) slabs spare ribs

Pineapple Chili Sauce (recipe follows)

Preheat the oven to 450°F.

Trim any large areas of excess fat and the membrane from the back of the ribs (page 90) and cut the ribs into individual serving pieces. Put the ribs in a shallow roasting pan, meat side down, and roast for 30 minutes. Remove from the oven and pour off any excess fat. Pour the Pineapple Chili Sauce over the ribs.

Lower the oven temperature to 350°F. Turn the ribs over and cover the roasting pan with aluminum foil. Return to the oven and cook for an additional 1½ hours, or until the meat pulls easily away from the bones, basting periodically with the sauce. Serve hot.

Pineapple Chili Sauce

yields 3 cups

½ fresh ripe pineapple, roughly chopped (about 2 cups)

1 tablespoon olive oil

1 medium sweet onion, finely diced

¼ cup rice vinegar

⅓ cup chili sauce

1 tablespoon freshly squeezed lemon juice

2 tablespoons Worcestershire sauce

1 tablespoon Dijon mustard

Kosher salt

Freshly ground black pepper

In a blender or food processor, puree the pineapple until it is nearly smooth.

Heat a medium saucepan over medium heat and add the oil. Stir in the onion and cook until it is translucent, about 5 minutes. Stir in the vinegar, chili sauce, lemon juice, Worcestershire sauce, and mustard, then add the pineapple puree and ½ cup water. Bring to a boil, lower the heat, and simmer for 10 minutes. Salt and pepper to taste.

Picnic Shoulder

arm picnic : arm roast : arm steak : ground pork : hock : sausage

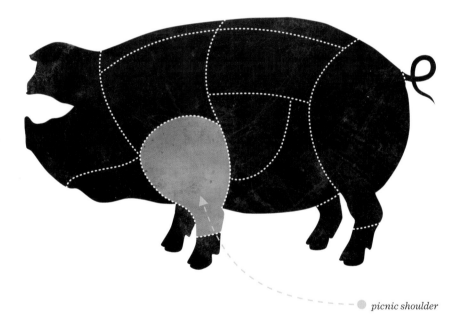

picnic shoulder

Sunday pot roast memories probably started with a picnic roast. The picnic shoulder is the lower, fattier section of the pig's front legs. Located just below the Boston shoulder, it is the upper part of the foreleg, and extends from the shoulder socket to the elbow. Because of its higher fat content, the picnic shoulder makes for juicy and flavorful roasts. Cuts from the picnic shoulder are not only flavorful but very affordable, and make the best fresh sausage because of the meat-to-fat ratio. The shoulder hocks make an imaginative osso buco, and when roasted, the neck bones make a rich, smooth stock that will add a depth of flavor to soups and stews.

Cooking Methods: Best when slow roasted or braised, and for making ground pork and sausage.

Lula Mae's Double Cola–Braised Pork Shoulder

My mom says I remind her of my grandma, Lula Mae. Grandma's chain-smoking habits aside, I take that as a compliment. Lula Mae was what you would call a "character." Grandma had a smile as wide as the Missouri River and an off-color vocabulary running nearly as long. She had hair that changed colors often, depending on what box was on sale at the corner drugstore, and I saw it in curlers more than out. Heck, she sometimes even slept with it all wrapped up in toilet paper! It was rare for me to be able to steal a private moment with Lula Mae. Taking care of a farm, a husband, and seven kids, she just didn't have enough time in the day to spare. By the time I came around, her kids and God knows how many grandkids had conspired to run her ragged. Funny thing is, she kept up just fine. Better than fine. She could slop pigs, split wood, and hand wash pantyhose all at the same time. Everyone would agree, though, that the thing she did best of all was cook. I wish I could say Grandma taught me how to cook, but that would be a lie. She did teach my mom how to cook, and I'm grateful for that.

I have two vivid childhood memories of Lula Mae that I treasure. The first is of me hiding under the kitchen table at her feet while she played hearts late into the night with my parents. I curled up by her bare feet—with those toes always painted red—and listened to her tell stories that I wouldn't understand until years later. All the same, I laughed under my breath just because everyone was whooping and hollering. Between Lula Mae and my father—both could make a story about a dying kitten the funniest thing you'd ever heard—my mom and grandfather couldn't get a word in edgewise. But seeing their hands slapping against their thighs and their feet stomping wildly, I knew they were having a good time, too.

The second vivid memory always comes rushing back to me when I make Grandma's dish: a simple pork shoulder slow-roasted on the stove. Her secret recipe involved her favorite Double Cola soda, of which she kept a private stash. One hot summer afternoon, I caught Grandma in the kitchen alone and snuck up behind her. She turned in surprise and looked down at me wearing next to nothing in the heat, my hair plastered to my forehead with sweat. That's when I saw she had two bottles of Double Cola in her hands—one for the pot and one for her. Without saying a word, she smiled and handed me the half-empty bottle she was drinking from. It was like she gave me the world. But she actually gave me so much more—a rare moment together that I'll always treasure.

When I make this simple country recipe, I think of both my grandma's fierce laughter and her quiet kindness. I can still see her christening that pork shoulder by pouring the last sip of our shared Double Cola over it, and smell the heady onions cooking in her cast-iron pot. She, wearing a handmade apron over a smart double-knit pant suit, and I, an inch to her right, wearing only my underwear and a Double Cola smile.

Lula Mae's Double Cola-Braised Pork Shoulder (page 96)

Lula Mae's Double Cola–Braised Pork Shoulder

sweet onion pan gravy : entrée : serves 6 to 8

1 (3- to 4-pound) bone-in fresh pork shoulder half (preferably an arm picnic)

2 cloves garlic, cut into slivers

Kosher salt

Freshly ground black pepper

2 tablespoons vegetable oil

1½ pounds sweet onions, cut into thick slices

2 (12-ounce) bottles Double Cola or your favorite cola (just no diet cola, please)

8 cups cooked rice

Preheat the oven to 325°F.

Using a sharp paring knife, score the fat and skin of the pork in a decorative crosshatch pattern and make slits all over the meat. Insert slivers of garlic into the slits. Pat the pork dry and season it liberally with salt and pepper.

Heat the oil in a large cast-iron Dutch oven until it is hot but not smoking. Brown the pork shoulder for 6 to 10 minutes on each side, turning occasionally. Remove the pork to a plate and set aside.

Put the onions in the Dutch oven and sauté for 5 minutes, or until they have softened and are golden in color. Add 1 teaspoon salt and continue to sauté the onions for 6 to 8 minutes more, until they have caramelized. Stir in the cola and return the pork to the Dutch oven. Cover with a tight-fitting lid and place the pot in the middle of the oven. Cook for 2½ to 3 hours, until the pork is easily pierced by a fork, then remove the pork to a serving dish and return the Dutch oven to the stovetop to make the gravy.

Boil the rendered juices and onions, stirring often, until the mixture has reduced to about 2 cups. Season with salt and pepper to taste. Slice the pork and serve it over rice, with the pan gravy and a cold bottle of Double Cola.

Grilled Summer Corn Soup

radish, sweet italian sausage | soup | serves 4 to 6

3 ears fresh summer corn, shucked and cleaned

1 tablespoon vegetable oil

1 tablespoon unsalted butter

½ cup crumbled loose sweet Italian sausage

3 scallions, chopped

4 cups pork stock (page 154)

1 tablespoon arrowroot or cornstarch

2 tablespoons rice vinegar

3 large radishes, thinly sliced

Kosher salt

Freshly ground black pepper

Sesame oil

Preheat a grill, or indoor grill pan, to hot.

Brush the ears of corn with oil and place them on the grill. Cook for 5 minutes, turning, until grill marks appear on all sides. (The corn kernels should still be a bit hard; you are merely adding color and grill flavor to the corn.) Remove the ears from the grill and let them cool. When they are cool, run a knife down the cobs to remove the kernels. Set the kernels aside.

In a medium saucepan over medium heat, cook the butter and sausage for 5 minutes, or until the sausage is lightly browned. Stir in the scallions and cook, stirring, for 2 minutes. Add the stock and bring to a simmer.

Meanwhile, combine the arrowroot with 2 tablespoons water in a small bowl. Add the mixture to the simmering broth and whisk for 30 seconds. Simmer for 5 minutes more, then stir in the vinegar, corn kernels, and radishes and cook to heat through. Salt and pepper to taste. Serve hot with a drizzle of sesame oil on top.

To remove kernels of corn from the cob without making too big a mess, place the cob in the hole of a Bundt pan to hold it while you are cutting down the sides with a sharp knife. The bundt pan will capture most of the corn that falls off the cob.

SAUSAGE

Apple Orchard Stew

smoked sausage, cabbage, leeks │ entrée │ serves 4

I started cooking a variation of this delightful stew years ago. If I were to write this recipe tomorrow, it would probably not be the same as the one you are reading now. Use this and your own larder as a guide. Like my husband, it's very forgiving.

2 tablespoons vegetable oil

1 pound Smithfield Smoked Sausage, cut into ½-inch pieces

1 tablespoon unsalted butter

1 sweet onion, chopped

1 leek (white part only), rinsed and thinly sliced

¼ teaspoon ground allspice

1 tablespoon all-purpose flour

3 cups pork stock (page 154)

1 cup apple cider

1 tablespoon Dijon mustard

2 cups shredded green cabbage

½ pound red potatoes, quartered

3 tart green apples, such as Granny Smith, unpeeled, seeded and cut into large chunks

2 tablespoons chopped fresh parsley

Kosher salt

Freshly ground black pepper

½ loaf day-old French bread, torn into thick pieces

Heat 1 tablespoon of the oil in a Dutch oven over medium-high heat. Stir in the sausage and cook for 3 minutes, until just browned around the edges. Transfer the sausage to a plate and set aside.

Lower the heat to medium-low, add the remaining oil, the butter, onion, leek, and allspice and cook for 3 minutes, or until the onions begin to soften. Stir in the flour and cook for 3 minutes, stirring constantly. Slowly stir in the stock, 1 cup water, the cider, and mustard, stirring until the mixture is well combined. Add the cabbage and potatoes, stir, and bring to a boil. Lower the heat and simmer, covered, for 15 minutes. Stir in the apples, cover, and cook for 10 minutes.

Just before serving, stir in the sausage, plus any juices that have accumulated on the plate, and the parsley. Salt and pepper to taste. Simmer gently for 2 minutes, until the sausage is heated through. Put pieces of the bread in the bottoms of four serving bowls, ladle the stew over the bread, and serve.

Hog-tied and Hungry Chili

jalapeño cheese dumplings · entrée · serves 6

Yee Holy Howdeedooda, this is good.

For the chili:

1 pound dried black beans, rinsed and drained

1 pound ground pork

1 large sweet onion, finely diced

2 cloves garlic, minced

2 (4½-ounce) cans chopped green chiles

1 chipotle chile in adobo sauce, minced

1 tablespoon chili powder

2 tablespoons ground cumin

1 teaspoon kosher salt

1 teaspoon freshly ground black pepper

1 (28-ounce) can crushed San Marzano tomatoes

2 cups tomato juice

2 cups pork stock (page 154)

2 ounces bittersweet chocolate, chopped

For the dumplings:

½ cup all-purpose flour

½ cup masa harina

1 teaspoon baking powder

½ teaspoon kosher salt

1 large egg

½ cup milk

1 tablespoon leaf lard (page 170) or vegetable shortening, melted

2 teaspoons honey

½ cup shredded cheddar cheese

1 jalapeño chile, seeded and minced

In a large stockpot, cover the beans with 3 inches of cold water. Bring to a boil, lower the heat, and simmer for 2 hours, or until the beans are fork tender. Drain the beans and set aside.

In the same large stockpot, cook the pork until the meat is no longer pink. Stir in the onion, garlic, green chiles, chipotle, chili powder, cumin, salt, and pepper. Sauté for 10 minutes, or until the onion is translucent. Stir in the beans, tomatoes, tomato juice, stock, and chocolate. Bring to a boil, then lower the heat and simmer for 30 minutes.

Meanwhile, make the dumplings: Whisk together the all-purpose flour, masa harina, baking powder, and salt in a large mixing bowl. In a separate mixing bowl, whisk together the egg, milk, lard, and honey. Stir the wet ingredients into the dry ingredients until just combined. Stir in the cheese and jalapeño.

Drop heaping tablespoons of the dumpling dough into the simmering chili, leaving a little space between the dumplings so they do not touch. Cover and simmer for 20 minutes. Do not lift the lid while the dumplings are cooking. The dumplings should be firm to the touch, but still moist in the center. Serve hot.

Hock and Beans

side : serves 4

One of the great things about pork is that you can use every part of the animal. Allowing nothing to go to waste is the respectful way to treat the beast. Parts like feet, fatback, clear plate, and hocks are the building-flavor-blocks for dishes like a simple pot of black beans. Without the hocks in this recipe it would be just fine. With the hocks . . . just fantastic.

1 pound dried black beans

2 tablespoons olive oil

1 medium sweet onion, diced

2 cloves garlic, smashed

1 teaspoon ground cumin

½ teaspoon dried oregano

1 (4-ounce) can diced green chiles

½ teaspoon kosher salt

½ teaspoon freshly ground black pepper

3 cups pork stock (page 154) or chicken stock

6 small whole tomatillos, husks removed

2 smoked pork hocks

Rinse the beans and soak them overnight in enough water to cover. Drain and set aside.

Heat the oil in a Dutch oven over medium-high heat. Stir in the onion, garlic, cumin, oregano, chiles, salt, and pepper and sauté for 5 minutes. Stir in the stock, 1 cup water, the tomatillos, and beans. Add the hocks. Bring to a boil, and continue to boil for 5 minutes. Lower the heat, cover, and simmer for 1 to 2 hours, until the beans are soft, but not mushy. If needed, add additional water or stock while the beans are simmering. Serve the hocks whole or shred the meat and stir it into the beans, discarding the bones.

For quick refried beans, drain the cooked beans of most of their liquid and mash with a potato masher. Heat 3 tablespoons bacon grease in a large cast-iron skillet and add the mashed beans. Fry for 3 to 4 minutes, stirring often. Makes a great accompaniment to Midnight Pork Tamales (page 42).

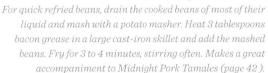

how to

Make Breakfast Sausage | yields 12 (4-inch) sausages

My goal for this little tutorial is to give you the kick in the butt you need to start making your own sausage. Once you see how easy this breakfast sausage technique is to master, I hope it inspires you to give it a go. No, I don't want you to move to a shack in the woods, forgo bathing, and say things like "I'm totally off the grid, man." I just want to give you another good reason to reach for the family farm–raised pork at your local farmers' market. Go ahead, take it home and make your own sausage. It's really this simple.

4 feet (1- to 1¼-inch-diameter) natural salted hog casings (see Source Guide, page 186)

1 tablespoon distilled white vinegar

1 tablespoon kosher salt

1 teaspoon freshly ground black pepper

1 teaspoon brown sugar

½ teaspoon dried thyme

½ teaspoon dried sage

Pinch of ground cloves

Pinch of cayenne pepper

2½ pounds lean fresh arm picnic roast, cut into 1-inch cubes and frozen for 30 minutes

8 ounces pork fat, cut into 1-inch cubes and frozen for 30 minutes

Stand mixer fitted with a grinder attachment (fine grinding disk) and sausage stuffer attachment

Baker's twine (optional)

1   Rinse the casings under running water and soak them in a container of cold water for 30 minutes. Rinse the casings a second time under running water. Fill the container with fresh cold water, stir in the vinegar, and return the casings to the container. (The vinegar helps to soften the casings and give them more of a transparent look when filled.) Combine the salt, black pepper, brown sugar, thyme, sage, cloves, and cayenne in a separate bowl. (This is where you can create your own flavor. Try a variety of seasonings and see what combinations you like the best.) Remove the meat and fat from the freezer.

2   Using a stand mixer on #4 speed and a meat grinder attachment with a fine disk, begin to feed the partially frozen meat and fat through the grinder's hopper. Have a clean bowl sitting under the grinder to catch the ground meat and fat as they come out.

3   Season the ground meat mixture with the spice mixture.

continued on page 106

I like to dress up my sausage by tying colorful baker's twine between the links. I believe everything, even sausage, should be properly accessorized.
(remove before cooking)

continued from page 104

how to

Make Breakfast Sausage | yields 12 (4-inch) sausages

4 Using your hands, mix the seasoning into the ground meat and fat until it is well combined. A good tip is to have a dish of ice water ready. Keeping your hands icy cold helps prevent the fat from sticking to them, and helps make cleaning up easier.

5 Attach the sausage stuffing attachment to your grinder and slide the soaked casings over the end. Leave 3 inches of casing hanging off the edge of the stuffer and tie a knot at the end of the casing.

6 Begin feeding the seasoned sausage mixture through the grinder's hopper until all the sausage mixture is used. Your stand mixer's speed should still be set on #4.

7 Inspect the sausage for air bubbles and use a pin or sausage perforator to prick any bubbles you find, releasing the air.

8 Starting with the tied end, twist the sausage into links by grasping the sausage every 4 inches with both hands and giving it two or three twists, with each hand twisting in the opposite direction (much like ringing out a dishtowel). Congratulations, you just made breakfast sausage!

Fat is a necessary ingredient in sausage. It helps bind the ingredients together and carries their flavor throughout the sausage. Without a small amount of fat, your sausage will become too dry. I like a 20 percent fat-to-lean-meat ratio. For the best fat, I ask my farmer to save me a piece of back fat. I trim off the rind (skin), and cut it into pieces to freeze for sausage making.

Stuffed Baked Apples

sweet italian sausage, apricots, maple syrup | side | serves 6

6 large tart baking apples

1 tablespoon freshly squeezed lemon juice

1 pound sweet Italian sausage, casings removed

2 tablespoons sweet onion, minced

1 garlic clove, minced

1 tablespoon finely chopped fresh parsley

1 tablespoon finely chopped fresh sage

⅓ cup dried apricots, soaked in water overnight and chopped

3 tablespoons brown sugar

¼ cup (½ stick) unsalted butter, at room temperature

Kosher salt

Freshly ground black pepper

1 large egg, beaten

4 slices smoked slab bacon, chopped

Warm maple syrup (optional)

Preheat the oven to 350°F.

Cut ½ inch off the top of each apple. Using a small serrated spoon or melon baller, remove the apple core, leaving only ½ inch of flesh around. Reserve and chop any flesh that was removed, discarding the cores. Slice a very small sliver off the bottom of each apple to allow it to sit in the baking dish without falling over. Brush the inside of the apples with lemon juice and put the apples, cored side up, in a 9-inch round baking dish.

In a large sauté pan over medium heat, cook the sausage, onion, and garlic, breaking the sausage apart with a spoon or spatula, until it is cooked through and light brown. Remove from the pan and drain. Put the drained sausage mixture in a large mixing bowl. Stir in the parsley, sage, apricots, 1 tablespoon of the brown sugar, the reserved chopped apple, and butter. Salt and pepper to taste. Stir in the egg. Stuff the apples with the sausage mixture, mounding the tops. Any remaining sausage mixture can be tossed into the baking dish around the apples or saved to add to your scrambled eggs the next morning. Sprinkle the tops with the remaining brown sugar and the bacon, cover with aluminum foil, and bake for 40 minutes, until the apples are soft; remove the foil for the final 5 minutes of baking so the bacon will crisp. Serve warm. Drizzle with maple syrup, if desired.

Never let a recipe limit you. Substitute any dried fruit you may have in your pantry. Figs, cranberries, and prunes all work great in this recipe in place of the apricots. Have some leftover stuffing from the holidays? Mix ½ cup stuffing into the cooked sausage mixture before baking.

Scottish Quail Eggs

tarragon mustard dipping sauce | appetizer | yields 20

Just another reason to watch TV.

I had never seen a Scotch egg until I saw Ewen MacIntosh's character, Keith, eat one on the BBC version of *The Office*. Then I became obsessed. Since that episode, I have been lucky enough to travel across the pond and sample Scotch eggs in my father's own motherland. I found that nearly all I sampled were a perfect size for Keith's gargantuan mouth, but way too big for the average piehole. I applied a little bit of bird-dog ingenuity and came up with the answer: Scottish Quail Eggs. A perfect fit for most mouths. The tarragon mustard sauce is just this American showing off.

20 quail eggs

1 tablespoon vinegar

1 teaspoon sea salt or kosher salt, plus more for sprinkling

1 pound freshly ground pork sausage (page 104) or pork breakfast sausage

2 cups all-purpose flour

4 large chicken eggs, beaten together with ¼ cup water

3 cups dried bread crumbs

Peanut oil for deep-frying

Tarragon Mustard Dipping Sauce (recipe follows)

Fill a large mixing bowl two-thirds full of ice water and set aside.

Carefully put the quail eggs in a medium saucepan and cover them with cold water. Add the vinegar and salt. Bring to a boil, immediately lower the heat, and simmer for 3 minutes. Drain the hot water from the eggs. Put the eggs in the ice water and let them cool completely, for 8 to 10 minutes. To peel the eggs, gently roll them on a hard surface to crack the shell all over. Beginning with the rounder end, peel off the shell. Be patient. Pat dry with a paper towel and set aside.

Line a baking sheet with waxed paper and set aside.

Have four bowls ready. Fill the first bowl with sausage, the second with flour, the third with beaten egg mixture, and the fourth with bread crumbs.

Flatten 1 heaping tablespoon of sausage into a disk in the palm of your hand. Dredge a hard-boiled quail egg in the flour. Shake off any excess flour. Place the egg in the center of the sausage disk and mold the sausage around it, making sure the entire egg is covered. Dip it into the egg mixture, then roll it in the bread crumbs. Put it on the prepared baking sheet and repeat with the remaining quail eggs. Chill the eggs for 30 minutes.

Tarragon Mustard Dipping Sauce

yields 1¼ cups

1 cup Dijon mustard

¼ cup Homemade Mayonnaise (page 80)

2 tablespoons chopped fresh tarragon

1 tablespoon rice vinegar

Kosher salt

Freshly ground black pepper

Line a baking sheet with paper towels and set aside.

Heat at least 4 inches of oil in a deep-fryer or Dutch oven to 360°F. Working in batches, gently slide the chilled eggs into the hot oil and fry for 3 to 4 minutes, turning, until golden brown. Remove the eggs to the paper towel–lined baking sheet to drain. Sprinkle with salt and serve with the sauce.

Combine the mustard, mayonnaise, tarragon, and vinegar in a small mixing bowl. Salt and pepper to taste.

GROUND PORK

Pork Hand Pies

....

potato, rutabaga │ entrée │ serves 4

....

I could call these "Chunnel" pies, as they are a cross between a French tortière and an English pasty. Eat them hot, warm, or cold, but frankly, they taste best out of a brown paper bag anytime you're hungry.

2 cups all-purpose flour

Kosher salt

Pinch of dry mustard powder

⅔ cup leaf lard (page 170) or vegetable shortening

12 ounces ground pork

3 cups diced potatoes

1 small sweet onion, diced

½ cup diced rutabaga

Pinch of ground ginger

Pinch of crumbled dried thyme

2 tablespoons dried parsley

½ teaspoon freshly ground pepper

Butt-Kickin' Ketchup (page 18)

In a large mixing bowl, whisk together the flour, a pinch of salt, and the mustard powder. Using two forks or a pastry blender, cut in the lard until the mixture resembles coarse meal. Add ½ cup water and knead the dough until it is well blended. Form the dough into 4 balls, cover, and refrigerate for 10 minutes.

Preheat the oven to 400°F.

In a large mixing bowl, combine pork, potatoes, onion, rutabaga, ginger, thyme, parsley, pepper, and 1 teaspoon salt.

To assemble the pork pies, on a heavily floured surface, roll out each of the dough balls into an 8- or 9-inch round. Divide the pork mixture into 4 equal portions and place a portion in the center of each crust. Fold over and decoratively crimp the edges of the dough to seal. Put the pork pies on a baking sheet and bake for 50 to 60 minutes, until golden brown. Serve hot, warm, or cold with Butt-Kickin' Ketchup.

clockwise from top left:
Pork Hand Pies,
Precious Sausage-Stuffed Deep-Fried Dills (page 112),
Sweet Potato Pork Pie (page 113)
Stuffed Baked Apples (page 107)

INSERT
FORK
HERE

Precious Sausage-Stuffed Deep-Fried Dills

sweet horseradish dipping sauce | appetizer | yields 12 to 18 pickles

Moving to rural North Carolina from the ever hip and haughty Vail, Colorado, was a lesson in the proper way to eat humble pie. I opened my heart and mind to things that were "precious"—a word that Southerners use interchangeably with the phrase "bless her heart." Hell, I even added the word *precious* to my vocabulary. I slowed down long enough to recognize that the bag of still-warm duck livers left on my doorstep by my duck-hunting neighbor was a precious gift, that being alone in a handmade canoe as dawn broke on the river was a precious moment. And discovering that the pickles you get on the side of your North Carolina barbecue are fried—now, that that was a precious surprise!

1 (46-ounce) jar whole dill pickles, drained and patted dry

½ pound hot Italian sausage, casings removed, chopped, and fully cooked

2 cups self-rising flour

1 tablespoon sugar

½ teaspoon kosher salt, plus more for sprinkling

¼ teaspoon freshly ground black pepper

½ cup buttermilk

1 cup Budweiser beer (or your choice beer)

½ teaspoon Texas Pete hot sauce

Peanut oil for deep-frying

Sweet Horseradish Dipping Sauce (recipe follows)

Slice ¼ inch off both ends of each pickle. Working on one end of each pickle at a time, use a paring knife (working it like a corkscrew) to carefully hollow out half of the pickle. Repeat from the other end. Transfer the insides to a cutting board and finely chop.

In a medium mixing bowl, stir together the finely chopped pickles and the sausage. Stuff each hollow pickle with the sausage mixture and set aside.

In a medium mixing bowl, whisk together 1 cup of the flour, the sugar, salt, and pepper. Whisk in the buttermilk, beer, and hot sauce and continue whisking until the batter is smooth. Let the mixture sit at room temperature while the oil is heating.

Heat the oil in a Dutch oven or deep-fryer to 360°F. Line a baking sheet with paper towels and set aside.

Pour the remaining flour into a medium mixing bowl. Working in small batches, dredge the stuffed pickles in the flour and shake off any excess. Dip the floured pickles into the batter and shake off any excess. Gently slide the pickles into the hot oil and cook until lightly browned. Remove to the prepared baking sheet to drain. Sprinkle with salt while the pickles are hot. Serve warm with Sweet Horseradish Dipping Sauce.

Sweet Horseradish Dipping Sauce

yields scant 2 ½ cups

2 cups sour cream

¼ cup honey

3 tablespoons prepared horseradish

Pinch of kosher salt

Combine all the ingredients in a small mixing bowl and stir well. The sauce will keep, refrigerated, for 1 week.

For a more pungent flavor, prepare the Sweet Horseradish Dipping Sauce a day ahead.

Sweet Potato Pork Pie

entrée | serves 6

1 pound ground pork

1 large onion, chopped

1 tablespoon balsamic vinegar

1 teaspoon kosher salt

½ teaspoon freshly ground black pepper

¼ teaspoon ground cinnamon

⅛ teaspoon ground cloves

3 sweet potatoes, boiled, peeled, and mashed

½ cup Applesauce (page 23)

2 tablespoons chopped fresh flat-leaf parsley

Way Better Than Basic Pie Dough, double crust (page 167)

1 large egg

In a large saucepan over medium-low heat, combine the pork, onion, vinegar, salt, pepper, and ¼ cup water. Simmer until the pork is no longer pink. Remove from the heat and stir in the cinnamon, cloves, sweet potatoes, applesauce, and parsley. Let the mixture cool while you roll out the pie dough.

Preheat the oven to 425°F.

On a lightly floured surface, roll out a round of dough to a 12-inch circle. Drape it over a 9-inch pie plate, allowing it to fall naturally into the plate. Do not stretch the dough. Fill the pie with the pork mixture and set aside. Roll out the second round of dough to an 11-inch circle and drape it over the top of the pie. Trim the edges and decoratively crimp.

Make an egg wash by beating the egg together with 1 tablespoon water. Cut four vents in the top of the pie and brush the top of the pie with the egg wash. Bake for 30 minutes, until the crust is golden brown. Slice and serve.

Spicy Meatballs and Simple Sunday Red Sauce

hot italian sausage, pork chop seasoned sauce ┊ entrée ┊ serves 6 to 8

My first husband, John, was a chef, a worrier, and a friend. He gave me my dearest treasure, our son Anthony, and the inspiration for this simple red sauce. I gave him a headache.

2 tablespoons olive oil

1 large onion, diced

3 cloves garlic, diced

1 tablespoon chopped fresh oregano

Pinch of ground cinnamon

Kosher salt

Freshly ground black pepper

2 (½-inch-thick) bone-in pork chops

3 (28-ounce) cans crushed San Marzano tomatoes

2 bay leaves

Spicy Meatballs (recipe follows)

2 pounds thin spaghetti, cooked al dente

Freshly grated Parmesan cheese

Chopped fresh parsley

Heat the oil in a large Dutch oven over medium-low heat. Add the onion, garlic, oregano, cinnamon, 2 teaspoons salt, and ½ teaspoons pepper and cook, stirring often, for 15 minutes, or until the onion is translucent. Add the pork chops and cook for 5 minutes, turning once. Stir in the tomatoes and bay leaves. Fill one of the empty tomato cans with water and stir the water into the sauce. Bring to a low boil, then stir, cover, and lower the heat to low. Simmer over low heat, stirring occasionally, for 4 hours, until the pork falls from the bone. Remove the bones and season with salt and pepper to taste.

Carefully place the meatballs in the sauce. Simmer for 10 minutes. Serve hot over the spaghetti, sprinkled with cheese and parsley.

To reheat the meatballs, add the sauce and meatballs to a large sauté pan. Cook over medium-low heat until the meatballs are heated through.

Spicy Meatballs

yields 16

1 tablespoon olive oil

1 medium onion, finely diced

2 cloves garlic, minced

2 teaspoons chopped fresh oregano

$\frac{1}{2}$ cup milk

3 slices white bread

1 pound hot Italian sausage, casings removed, chopped

1 pound ground veal

1 pound ground chuck

1 large egg, lightly beaten

2 tablespoons chopped fresh parsley

$\frac{1}{2}$ cup finely grated Parmesan cheese

$1\frac{1}{2}$ teaspoons kosher salt

1 teaspoon freshly ground black pepper

Preheat the oven to 350°F. Grease a baking sheet and set aside.

Heat the oil in a large sauté pan over medium heat. Stir in the onion, garlic, and oregano and cook for 15 minutes, stirring often, until the onion is translucent. Remove from the heat and let the mixture cool.

Put the milk in a shallow bowl. Submerge the bread in the milk to soak. Remove the bread and squeeze out any extra milk. Tear the bread into small pieces. In a large mixing bowl, combine the soaked bread, sausage, veal, chuck, cooled onion-garlic mixture, egg, parsley, cheese, salt, and pepper. Mix with your hands, then divide the mixture into 16 portions and shape into 2-inch meatballs. Put the meatballs on the prepared baking sheet and bake for 20 minutes.

Bayou Pork Burger Sliders

creole mayo | appetizer or entrée | yields 20 sliders

I've had exotic burgers all over the world, and for the most part they all have one thing in common: They taste like chicken. In Florida, a gator burger . . . a tough chicken. In Peru, a guinea-pig burger . . . a cute chicken. In Honduras, an iguana burger . . . a funky chicken. I was finally ready for a nonbeef burger that tasted like something other than chicken. Bayou Pork Burger Sliders taste like pork!

1 tablespoon olive oil

1 medium sweet onion, finely chopped

2 cloves garlic, minced

1 red bell pepper, finely chopped

2 teaspoons Creole Seasoning (recipe follows)

2 pounds ground pork

1 large egg

½ cup dried bread crumbs

20 slider buns

Creole Mayonnaise (recipe follows)

Heat the oil in a medium sauté pan over medium-low heat and stir in the onion, garlic, pepper, and Creole Seasoning. Sauté for 6 to 8 minutes, until the onion is translucent.

Transfer to a large mixing bowl and let cool completely. Add pork, egg and bread crumbs and mix with your hands until combined. Divide the mixture into 20 portions and shape each into a small patty (no larger than your slider buns).

Grease a large skillet and cook sliders over medium heat for 3 to 4 minutes per side, until lightly browned and cooked through. Place each slider on the bottom half of a bun. Top with a dollop of Creole Mayonnaise and the top half of the bun. Serve warm or at room temperature.

Creole Seasoning can be stored in an airtight container in a cool, dark pantry for up to 3 months.

Creole Seasoning

yields ⅞ cup

3 tablespoons paprika

2 tablespoons garlic powder

2 tablespoons onion powder

1 tablespoon kosher salt

1 tablespoon celery salt

1 tablespoon cayenne pepper

1 tablespoon freshly ground black pepper

1 tablespoon dried oregano

1 tablespoon dried thyme

1 tablespoon dried basil

Combine all the ingredients in a bowl.

Creole Mayo

yields 1 cup

1 cup Homemade Mayonnaise (page 80)

1 teaspoon Creole Seasoning (recipe at left)

Juice of 1 lemon

1 tablespoon minced fresh chives

In a medium mixing bowl, combine all the ingredients.

Charcuterie

The French have a saying
"Tout est bon dans le cochon."
Roughly translated, it means
everything is good in a pig.
The craft of charcuterie
celebrates this saying.
Preserving meat by salting,
curing, and smoking . . .
nothing goes to waste.

clockwise from top left:
Capicola, mortadella, pepperoni,
Spanish chorizo, summer sausage,
red pepper salami, smoked sausage,
saucisson sec

Sweet Tea–Brined Pork Roast

lemon mint mashed potatoes : entrée : serves 8

"Y'all wan' some tea?" Sit down in any family restaurant in the South, and that's probably the first thing you will hear. This recipe is a respectful payback to every wonderful sweet-tea drinker I've ever shared a pitcher with.

2 (family-size) tea bags

1 cup sugar

⅓ cup kosher salt

2 lemons, zested and sliced

4 cups ice

1 (4-pound) pork arm roast, fresh arm picnic, or Boston blade roast

Lemon Mint Mashed Potatoes (recipe follows)

In a large saucepan over high heat, bring 4 cups cold water to a boil. Remove from the heat and add the tea bags. Let tea steep for 10 minutes, then remove the bags (be sure to press all the liquid from the bags). Heat the tea over low heat. Whisk in the sugar and keep whisking until it dissolves. Whisk in the salt, whisking until it dissolves. Add the lemon zest and slices and simmer for 5 minutes. Remove from the heat and stir in the ice. Refrigerate and let the brine cool completely.

Using a sharp knife, score a diamond pattern onto the top of the pork roast; the cuts should be no more than ½ inch deep. Put the pork in a large nonreactive bowl and pour the cold tea brine over it. Cover with plastic wrap and refrigerate for 24 hours.

Preheat the oven to 350°F.

Drain the pork and pat it dry. Put the pork in a shallow roasting pan and cover with aluminum foil. Bake for 2 hours, or until the internal temperature of the meat is 160°F. Let the roast rest for 15 minutes before slicing. Slice and serve with Lemon Mint Mashed potatoes.

Using the family-sized tea bags makes a very strong tea, which is needed to impart just a subtle flavor to the pork roast. If you don't have family-size tea bags, use 8 regular-size bags.

Lemon Mint Mashed Potatoes

yields 6 cups

3 pounds Yukon Gold potatoes, peeled and quartered

1 teaspoon kosher salt, plus more for sprinkling

½ cup heavy cream

¼ cup (½ stick) unsalted butter

1 tablespoon chopped white chocolate

Freshly ground black pepper

2 tablespoons grated lemon zest

2 tablespoons chopped fresh mint

Put the potatoes in a large pot and cover with cold water. Add the 1 teaspoon salt to the water and bring to a boil. Lower the heat and simmer, covered, for 15 to 20 minutes, until the potatoes can be easily pierced with a fork.

In a small saucepan, heat the cream and butter just until the butter has melted. Drain the potatoes and return them to the pot. Add the cream mixture and the white chocolate. Using a potato masher, mash the potato mixture to your desired consistency. Salt and pepper to taste. Stir in the lemon zest and mint. Serve with Sweet Tea–Brined Pork Roast.

The pasture-raised heritage pigs at Caw Caw Creek farm in South Carolina love white chocolate. I even got to feed some a few of the sweet chips on my last visit. This was the inspiration for the white chocolate in my mashed potatoes. It's a very subtle flavor that makes the pork roast a standout dish. Guests at your dinner table will know there's a secret ingredient in the potatoes that are making them taste fabulous, but they'll never be able to put their finger on it! White chocolate is also a wonderful addition to your mashed potatoes when you are serving lamb.

Pork Osso Buco

orange gremolata | entrée | serves 4

I don't need Carl Jung or a Myers-Briggs test to discern the personality types of any new guests at my dinner table. I just serve osso buco. Its marrow, I've found, is the true measure of type. Once I present the dish, I quietly observe how each guest handles the marrow. Those who dive right in and eat the marrow first: Type A. Those who savor the dish and save the marrow for last: Type B. Those who leave it on their plate untouched . . . not invited back.

4 (1¼- to 1½-pound) pork shanks

Kosher salt

Freshly ground black pepper

2 tablespoons olive oil

2 tablespoons unsalted butter

¾ cup diced sweet onion

¾ cup diced celery heart

¾ cup diced carrots

1 leek (white part only), rinsed and chopped

2 cloves garlic, minced

1 cup dry white wine

Grated zest and juice of 1 orange

Grated zest and juice of 1 lemon

1 cup canned crushed tomatoes

2 cups pork stock (page 154), heated

1 bay leaf

2 tablespoons fresh thyme leaves

4 fresh parsley sprigs

Orange Gremolata (recipe follows)

4 cups hot cooked yellow grits

Preheat the oven to 325°F.

Season the pork shanks liberally with salt and pepper.

Heat the oil and butter in a Dutch oven over high heat. When the oil is hot, but not smoking, sear the pork shanks on all sides for 10 minutes, until well browned. Remove the pork shanks to a plate and set aside.

Put the onion, celery heart, carrots, leek, and garlic in the Dutch oven and sauté for 3 to 4 minutes. Add the wine to deglaze the pan, being sure to scrape up all the browned bits from the bottom. Stir in the orange and lemon zest and juice and simmer for 5 minutes. Stir in the tomatoes and bring to a boil. Return the shanks to the Dutch oven. Add the stock, bay leaf, thyme, and parsley. Salt and pepper to taste. Cover and place the pot in the middle of the oven; cook for 2½ hours, or until the shanks are fork tender and the meat is beginning to separate from the bone. The vegetable mixture will now be a rich sauce. Remove the shanks from the sauce and set aside.

Stir the Orange Gremolata into the sauce and cover. Let both the shanks and the sauce rest for 10 minutes before serving. Serve the pork shanks over hot grits and spoon the sauce liberally over the top.

Orange Gremolata

yields ½ cup

½ cup minced flat-leaf parsley

1 tablespoon grated orange zest

1 tablespoon grated lemon zest

2 cloves garlic, minced

Combine all the ingredients in a small mixing bowl and stir well.

Spanish-Style Rioja Potatoes

russets, paprika, chorizo | side | serves 4

The only things I brought home from my first trip to Spain were a love letter and the biggest can of pimentón (smoked paprika) I could fit in my backpack. I still have the can that held the pimentón. It's long since been empty of spice, but safe inside is the first, last, and only love letter I received from my Spanish admirer. The aftershave aroma has been replaced with a smoky memory.

¼ cup olive oil

1 shallot, thinly sliced

1 small onion, thinly sliced

1 tablespoon smoked paprika

3 pounds russet potatoes, peeled and cut into 2-inch pieces

1 small hot red pepper, cut in half

1 green bell pepper, seeded and cut into large pieces

1 cup roughly chopped Spanish chorizo

Kosher salt

Freshly ground black pepper

Crusty bread

Heat the oil in a large heavy skillet over medium heat. Stir in the shallot, onion, and paprika. Cook for 5 minutes, until the onion is soft. Add the potatoes and stir to coat. Cook for 5 minutes. Add the red pepper, bell pepper, and 2 cups water. Stir and bring to a boil, then lower the heat and simmer for 10 minutes.

Stir in the chorizo and cook for 20 to 25 minutes, until the potatoes are tender. Remove from the heat and let the mixture rest for 10 minutes. The cooking liquid will have the thickness of a sauce. Salt and pepper to taste. Serve with bread for sopping.

6

Leg

ham shank ┊ ham butt ┊ center ham slice ┊ ham hock

leg

The hind legs of a pig provide fresh ham that can be left whole or divided into a ham shank (the lower section of the leg), or a ham butt (the upper section of the leg). Ham hocks are the shin, calf, and other muscles, bones, fat, and skin cut from just above the knee to the ankle on the hind legs. They are most often sold smoked, and really pump up the flavor when added to vegetables, soups, and stews.

Cooking Methods: Hams can be smoked or cured. Country ham, serrano, and prosciutto are all made from hams that are cured, smoked, and left to air dry. Fresh hams are best when brined (to add moisture and flavor) and roasted. When sliced into steaks, the leg can either be pan-broiled or pan-fried.

Setsuko's Ham Fried Rice

Growing up in a small Missouri town, I always felt very cosmopolitan when my Japanese aunt, Setsuko, would come for a visit. My uncle Howard and she met in Japan when she was a young girl, soon married over the protests of her family, and moved to the United States. A week before her visits, our house would be abuzz with preparations, as if Jackie Onassis herself were coming. To me, Setsuko was even better than Jackie. She was the first "celebrity" I ever knew. Setsuko was the Madonna of my time; she needed three assistants just to schlep all of her things: clothes, wigs, rice steamer, sheets (yes, she traveled with her own), and a multitude of jars containing fishy-looking things floating in brine. My two older sisters and I were happy to oblige. Truth be known, I guess I was hoping that some of her international cool would rub off on me.

The highlight of Setsuko's visits was when my mom graciously allowed her to take over the kitchen (no small accomplishment considering mom guarded her kitchen as if it housed the secrets of the universe). I was underfoot the entire time. Setsuko explained to me through sign (she spoke little English) that Japanese cooking was simple and clean—unlike Chinese cooking, which for reasons I couldn't understand at the time, got her all worked up. For a long time, I snubbed Chinese cooking out of allegiance to Setsuko. As her nimble fingers worked to devein shrimp, she mumbled things in Japanese under her breath and, as if agreeing with herself, nodded so vigorously that her wiglet nearly came off.

Not wanting to disappoint Aunt Setsuko, I tried everything she made, even though the fishy stuff in the jars was not my favorite. At the time, my palate was as underdeveloped as my chest. But on each of her visits I begged her to make ham fried rice, to which she'd coyly respond, "Really? It so easy." But it had everything a kid wanted: tasty flavors, showy moves, and a fast delivery time.

Just a few years ago, Setsuko visited my own home for Thanksgiving. She moves just a little slower now, but still travels with enough luggage that I checked the driveway half expecting to see that she had chartered her own bus. We had a wonderful visit, but before she left, I threatened to hold her luggage hostage unless she taught me that recipe for ham fried rice. She appeared startled when I asked (apparently the word *hostage* was a little ominous), so I explained to her how important she and the dish were to me. She looked at me, smiled, nodded, and said, "Really? It so easy."

Setsuko's Ham Fried Rice (page 128)

Setsuko's Ham Fried Rice

scallion, egg · side · serves 4

2 tablespoons sesame oil

3 large eggs, beaten

1 clove garlic, minced

½ cup diced sweet onion

½ cup finely diced carrots

2 teaspoons Japanese mirin

**1 cup diced boneless
fully cooked smoked ham**

3 cups cooked rice, cooled

2 teaspoons white pepper

3 scallions, chopped

Japanese soy sauce

Heat a wok over very high heat. Add 1 tablespoon of the sesame oil and stir. Stir in the eggs and cook for 30 seconds, until loosely scrambled. Remove the eggs to a plate and set aside. Add the remaining sesame oil to the wok. Stir in the garlic, onion, carrots, and mirin. Cook, stirring, for 1 minute, or until the onion starts to brown. Stir in the ham and cook, stirring, for another minute. Return the eggs to the wok and stir to combine with the ham and vegetable mixture. Add the rice and white pepper and cook, stirring, for 30 seconds, until everything is well combined. Stir in the scallions and serve hot with soy sauce on the side.

Soy sauce can be stirred into the dish after the rice and white pepper, if you prefer. Use as much as you like for your personal tastes. Setsuko prefers to have everyone add his or her own.

LEG

Fresh Ham

entrée | serves 15

The best recipes are sometimes the ones with the fewest ingredients. This one is no exception.

1 (15-pound) pork leg, preferably pasture raised

1 cup organic tamari soy sauce

Let the pork leg sit at room temperature for 1 to 2 hours before cooking.

Preheat the oven to 325°F.

Trim any excess fat from the outside of the ham. Using a sharp knife, score the surface by cutting diamond patterns, ½ inch deep, into the ham. Put the ham in a large roasting pan and brush with ½ cup of the soy sauce, making sure to work it down into the cuts. Cover with aluminum foil and bake for 22 to 26 minutes per pound (5½ to 6½ hours for a 15-pound ham), until the internal temperature reaches 160°F. In the last hour of cooking, remove the foil and baste the ham with the remaining soy sauce. (Never baste a ham with its own renderings during cooking, as the renderings are usually very salty and will overpower the flavor of the meat.) Do not be alarmed if areas of the ham are getting a little black. This is due to the tamari soy sauce. You'll all be fighting for these crisp bits later! Remove the ham from the oven and let it rest for 15 minutes before slicing (page 130).

The soy sauce you choose for this recipe is key to its success. No matter what, it will be good if you choose a quality leg, but the right soy sauce will take it on a subtle taste trip over the top. A Japanese tamari is my choice, as it is made with more soybeans than average soy sauces. Thus, it is slightly thicker and has a more complex, smoky flavor. I also love how the tamari colors the ham a mahogany brown and black in some areas as it cooks.

how to

Here are simple carving techniques for getting every ounce of meat from your fresh cooked ham.

1 Fresh Ham (page 129), fully cooked, and allowed
to rest for at least 15 minutes

1 Put the whole ham on a cutting board with the shank (narrow end) to your right.

2 Using the meat fork to firmly hold the ham in place, cut horizontally along the top of the center bone. Do not cut all the way through to the end.

3 Starting at the shank end, cut vertically down, stopping at the horizontal cut.

4 Continue to cut vertical slices of your desired thickness until you near the other end of the ham.

5 Turn the ham over to the opposite side—what was formerly the underside—and repeat steps 2 through 4.

6 Turn the ham so that the shank end faces away from you and cut the remaining meat off either side of the bone, and slice.

7 You now have thickly sliced fresh ham and a ham bone. Save the ham bone to flavor soups and stews, or to make a pork stock (page 154).

opposite top left : Fresh Ham (page 129)

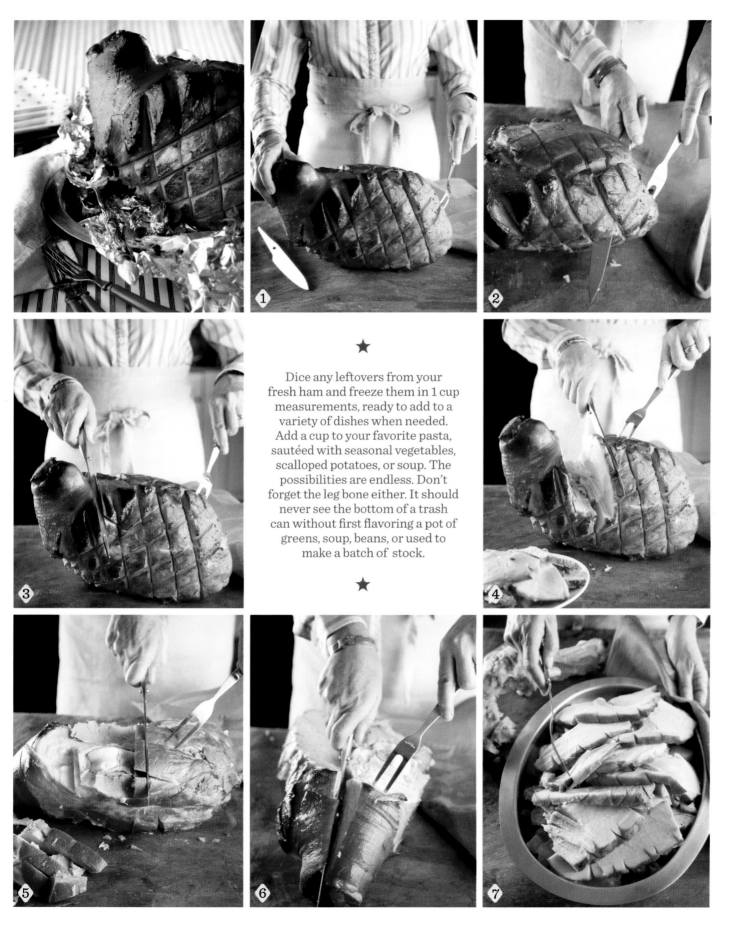

① ② ③ ④ ⑤ ⑥ ⑦

★

Dice any leftovers from your fresh ham and freeze them in 1 cup measurements, ready to add to a variety of dishes when needed. Add a cup to your favorite pasta, sautéed with seasonal vegetables, scalloped potatoes, or soup. The possibilities are endless. Don't forget the leg bone either. It should never see the bottom of a trash can without first flavoring a pot of greens, soup, beans, or used to make a batch of stock.

★

Buttery Potted Ham

mustard, tarragon | appetizer | serves 4 (yields 1 pint)

This is the adult version of the potted ham you loved as a kid. The crackers haven't changed.

1 cup (2 sticks) unsalted butter

½ pound fully cooked Smithfield ham, chopped

1 teaspoon Dijon mustard

¼ teaspoon freshly grated nutmeg

1 teaspoon chopped fresh tarragon, plus 1 whole leaf

Kosher salt

Freshly ground black pepper

Saltine crackers

Green Grass Refrigerator Pickles (page 50)

In a small saucepan, clarify the butter: Melt it over low heat, then remove from the heat and set aside for 5 minutes. Skim the froth from the top of the melted butter and pour the clear butter into a dish, discarding the milky solids left in the bottom of the pan. Transfer 3 tablespoons of the clarified butter to a small bowl and set aside.

Put the ham, mustard, nutmeg, chopped tarragon, and all the remaining clarified butter in a food processor and process until a smooth paste forms. Salt and pepper to taste. Pour the mixture into a clean 1-pint canning jar. Smooth the top and lay the tarragon leaf on top of the mixture. Pour the reserved clarified butter over the top, being sure to cover the potted ham and tarragon leaf completely, to create a seal. Cover with plastic wrap and refrigerate for 1 day before serving. Spread modestly on saltine crackers and serve with pickles. The potted ham will keep, refrigerated, for 7 days.

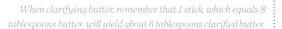

When clarifying butter, remember that 1 stick, which equals 8 tablespoons butter, will yield about 6 tablespoons clarified butter.

Quick Ham Bread

two-color olive butter | appetizer or side | serves 6

Quick breads are breads baked without yeast, typically dense, moist and the perfect 8-by-4-inch refuge for leftovers. In this delectable case, what was left over from last night's ham dinner is this afternoon's ham bread.

1⅔ cups all-purpose flour

½ teaspoon kosher salt

3 teaspoons baking powder

¼ teaspoon cayenne pepper

4 large eggs

½ cup milk

6 tablespoons olive oil

1 cup boneless smoked ham, finely chopped

¾ cup shredded Gruyère cheese

Two-Color Olive Butter (recipe follows)

Preheat the oven to 400°F. Grease one 8½-by-4½-inch loaf pan and set aside.

In a large mixing bowl, whisk together the flour, salt, baking powder, and cayenne.

In a medium mixing bowl, whisk together the eggs, milk, and oil. Stir in the chopped ham. Add the egg mixture to the flour mixture and stir until just combined. Fold in the cheese and pour the batter into the prepared pan. Bake for 10 minutes. Lower the oven temperature to 375°F and continue to bake for 30 to 40 minutes, until golden brown. Transfer the pan to a cooling rack and let cool for 5 minutes before turning the loaf out of the pan. Serve warm with Two-Color Olive Butter.

Two-Color Olive Butter

yields ½ cup

1 tablespoon finely chopped green olives

1 tablespoon finely chopped black olives

1 stick (½ cup) unsalted butter, softened

In a small mixing bowl, add all ingredients and stir until combined.

Super Mac and Cheese

side | serves 6

A Mac and Cheese Senryu

Intertwined elbows,
three pigs and four cows to make,
tastes like coming home.

7 tablespoons unsalted butter,
at room temperature

⅓ cup all-purpose flour

2⅔ cups milk

¾ cup shredded Gruyère cheese

½ cup freshly grated Parmesan cheese

½ cup shredded extra-sharp cheddar cheese

4 ounces cream cheese

6 cups cooked elbow macaroni
(about 3 cups uncooked)

¼ teaspoon kosher salt

1 teaspoon Texas Pete hot sauce

½ cup diced center smoked ham

4 ounces bacon, cooked crisp and chopped

4 ounces hot Italian sausage,
casing removed, cooked and chopped

½ cup crushed butter crackers

Preheat the oven to 375°F. Grease a 3-quart casserole dish and set aside.

In a large saucepan over medium heat, melt 5 tablespoons of the butter. Whisk in the flour and cook, stirring, for 3 minutes, until the mixture is blended and the flour gives off a nutty scent. Gradually whisk in the milk and cook, whisking constantly, until the mixture thickens. Stir in the cheeses and continue stirring until all the cheese has melted. Remove from the heat and stir in the macaroni, salt, hot sauce, ham, bacon, and sausage. Spoon the mixture into the prepared casserole dish.

In a small bowl, stir together the crackers and the remaining 2 tablespoons butter. Sprinkle over the macaroni mixture and bake for 30 minutes, or until golden and bubbly. Remove from the oven and let cool for 10 minutes before serving.

Prosciutto Pretzel Knots

stout mustard · appetizer · yields 20

No need to pour yourself a pint of beer to go with these stout-infused prosciutto pretzels and lapping mustard—but it won't hurt.

1 packet active dry yeast

1½ cups warm milk

1 tablespoon sugar

3½ cups all-purpose flour

1 teaspoon kosher salt

4 ounces prosciutto, chopped

1 tablespoon olive oil

12-ounces Guinness Pub Draught or other stout beer

2 tablespoons baking soda

1 large egg, beaten together with 1 tablespoon water

Coarse salt

Stout Mustard (recipe follows)

In a large mixing bowl, combine the yeast, milk, and sugar and set aside for 10 minutes, or until it foams.

In a food processor, combine the flour and kosher salt. With the motor running, slowly add the yeast mixture until just combined. Add the prosciutto and pulse until the dough forms a ball and cleans the sides of the work bowl. Drizzle the large mixing bowl with the oil and put the dough ball inside. Oil the top of the dough ball, cover the bowl with a cloth, and let the dough rise for 1 hour, until it has doubled in size.

Grease a baking sheet and set aside.

Punch the dough down with your fist and divide it into 20 balls. Roll each ball into a 5-inch-long rope and tie into a loose knot. Put the pretzel knots on the prepared baking sheet and let them rise for 20 to 30 minutes, until nearly doubled in size.

Preheat the oven to 400°F. Place a cooling rack atop a baking sheet and set aside. Line a baking sheet with parchment paper and set aside.

In a large, deep pan, bring 6 cups water, the beer, and baking soda to a low boil. Slide 2 or 3 pretzel knots at a time into the stout water and cook for 30 seconds per side, flipping the pretzels gently. Remove with a slotted spoon to the cooling rack to drain. Place the drained pretzels on the parchment-lined baking sheet. Brush them with the egg wash, and sprinkle them lightly with coarse salt. Bake for 12 to 15 minutes, until golden brown. Serve warm with the Stout Mustard.

Stout Mustard

yields 4 cups

12-ounces Guinness Pub Draught or other stout beer

1 ½ cups yellow mustard seeds

1 cup cider vinegar

1 tablespoon kosher salt

1 teaspoon freshly ground black pepper

½ teaspoon ground allspice

Pinch of freshly grated nutmeg

Put all the ingredients in a nonreactive mixing bowl, cover with plastic wrap, and let sit at room temperature overnight.

Transfer the mixture to a food processor and pulse until it thickens. Use immediately, or refrigerate for up to 1 month.

clockwise from top left:
Prosciutto Pretzel Knots ,
Prosciutto Parsnip Tots (page 139),
Super Mac and Cheese (page 135),
Quick Ham Bread (page 134)

Ham and Two-Cheese Drop Biscuits

garden butter | side | yields 12

2¼ cups self-rising flour

1 teaspoon kosher salt

6 tablespoons unsalted butter, chilled and diced

1 cup center smoked ham slice, finely diced

1½ cups finely shredded cheddar cheese

1 cup buttermilk, shaken well

¼ cup freshly grated Parmesan cheese

Garden Butter (recipe follows)

Preheat the oven to 450°F. Line a baking sheet with parchment paper and set aside.

In a large mixing bowl, whisk together the flour and salt. Cut in the butter using two forks or your fingers until the mixture resembles very coarse meal. Stir in the ham and cheddar cheese. Make a well in the middle of the ingredients and pour in the buttermilk. Stir until the mixture is just combined. Do not overwork the dough. Using a portion scoop or ¼-cup measure, drop 12 mounds of dough 2 inches apart onto the prepared baking sheet. Bake in the middle of the oven for 18 to 20 minutes, until the biscuits are golden. Remove from the oven and sprinkle the tops with the Parmesan cheese. Serve warm with Garden Butter.

Garden Butter

yields ½ cup

½ cup (1 stick) unsalted butter, at room temperature

1 clove garlic, minced

1 teaspoon minced fresh tarragon

1 teaspoon minced fresh thyme

1 teaspoon minced fresh rosemary

Combine all the ingredients in a small mixing bowl and stir well.

No rules apply to compound butter. Use whatever herbs you have growing in your garden.

Prosciutto Parsnip Tots

appetizer or side · serves 4

This ain't no grade-school cafeteria tot. This tot is all grown up and gone off to culinary school.

1 pound parsnips, peeled and cut into 1-inch pieces

2 cloves garlic, peeled and smashed

2 teaspoons fine sea salt

2 tablespoons unsalted butter

2 tablespoons heavy cream

¼ teaspoon freshly grated nutmeg

3 large eggs

2 tablespoons chopped fresh flat-leaf parsley

4 ounces prosciutto, chopped

2 tablespoons plus 1 cup all-purpose flour

Peanut oil for deep-frying

2 cups panko bread crumbs

Butt-Kickin' Ketchup (page 18)

In a large saucepan, combine the parsnips and garlic and cover with cold water. Add 1 teaspoon of the salt and bring to a boil, then lower the heat and simmer for 10 to 15 minutes, until the parsnips are fork tender. Drain, and put the parsnips and garlic in a large mixing bowl.

Using a hand mixer, beat the butter, cream, nutmeg, and remaining salt into the parsnip mixture. Beat in 1 of the eggs, the parsley, and prosciutto. Beat in 2 tablespoons of the flour. The mixture should be stiff.

Heat 4 inches of oil in a deep-fryer or Dutch oven to 360°F. Preheat the oven to 350°F. Line a baking sheet with parchment paper and set aside. Line a second baking sheet with paper towels and set aside.

Put the remaining flour in a small bowl. In another small bowl, beat the remaining eggs. Put the panko in a medium bowl.

Shape the parsnip mixture into 1½-inch balls, then roll and flatten them slightly to form cylinders. Dredge the parsnip tots first in the flour, then the eggs, and finally in the panko. Using a slotted metal spoon or the basket of the deep-fryer, gently lower the parsnip tots into the hot oil in batches and fry until golden brown. Remove and drain the tots on the paper towel–lined baking sheet. Transfer the drained parsnip tots to the parchment-lined baking sheet and bake for 15 minutes. Serve hot with Butt-Kickin' Ketchup.

Country Ham and Buttermilk Biscuits

clementine prosecco marmalade | entrée or side | ham serves 24

I am told my annual spring country ham and biscuit breakfast party is a coveted ticket in Savannah. You see, this isn't any "drop in" morning hoedown as the name suggests, it's a highly choreographed event. Seating times go out with the custom invitations. Eager guests know they don't show up early—or late—to this party, they show up on time. I'm not usually so militant about my soirees, but when hot biscuits and country ham are involved, people better get to steppin'. We have a blast with four seatings of six people (dogs are welcome, cats . . . not so much). The star of the show (the Smithfield country ham) sits proudly in the middle of the table, and my guests cut off pieces as they need them. Hot buttermilk biscuits dot every corner of the table, and each year there's a special fruit butter and preserve offered. This year it was blackberry butter and Clementine Prosecco Marmalade. The party is a great way to celebrate spring and the pig. Each hour is filled with friends' laughter and wonderful food. I even have boxes printed up so that each guest can take a piece of country ham home to season a pot of simmering beans or vegetables.

1 (12- to 16-pound) Smithfield Country Ham, uncooked

2 bay leaves

10 black peppercorns

¼ cup brown sugar

¼ cup dry mustard powder

Warm Buttermilk Biscuits (recipe follows)

Clementine Prosecco Marmalade (recipe follows)

I make a commitment when I cook a country ham. A commitment to myself and to the pig to use every piece of this wonderfully flavored meat and bone. I'll cut off a piece of the cooked meat and drop it into a pot of simmering vegetables, beans, or soup for seasoning. I make country ham dips and ham balls, and if you haven't had a piece of country ham smothered in red eye gravy, you haven't lived.

Begin 2 days before cooking. Using a stiff brush under warm running water, remove any surface mold that is present on the ham. (This mold is not a bad thing; during the process of aging, mold will grow naturally on the exterior of the ham. It is not injurious.) Put the ham in a large pot and cover completely with cold water. Let the ham soak at room temperature, changing the water every 4 to 8 hours. After 2 days of soaking, the ham is ready to cook.

In a large pot on the stovetop, put the ham skin side down and cover with fresh water. Add the bay leaves and peppercorns. Bring to a simmer and simmer, uncovered, for 25 minutes per pound (5 hours to 6 hours and 20 minutes), or until the internal temperature of the ham reaches 160°F. Add water as needed to keep the ham covered. When the ham is fully cooked, remove it from the pot and trim off any excess fat or skin, leaving at least a ¼-inch layer of fat on the ham. Never cut into the meat while trimming.

Preheat the oven to 400°F. In a small mixing bowl, stir together the brown sugar and mustard powder. Rub the outside of the ham with the mixture. Bake for 15 minutes, or until browned. Let the ham rest for 15 minutes before carving. Thinly slice and serve the ham on warm Buttermilk Biscuits with Clementine Prosecco Marmalade. For an added layer of crunch, fry the ham slices in a cast-iron skillet for 3 to 5 minutes on each side before serving. Freeze the leftover ham, tightly wrapped, for up to 3 months.

continued on page 142

continued from page 140

Buttermilk Biscuits

yields 9

1 ½ cups all-purpose flour

2 teaspoons baking powder

¼ teaspoon baking soda

1 teaspoon sugar

½ teaspoon kosher salt

¼ cup cold leaf lard (page 142) or vegetable shortening

½ cup buttermilk, or more as needed

2 tablespoons unsalted butter, melted

Preheat the oven to 450°F. Line a baking sheet with parchment paper and set aside.

In a medium mixing bowl, whisk together the flour, baking powder, baking soda, sugar, and salt. Using two forks or your fingers, work in the lard until the mixture begins to resemble coarse meal. Make a well in the center of the mixture and pour in the buttermilk. Stir until just moistened. The dough should come together at this point, but if necessary, add more buttermilk as needed. Turn the dough out onto a lightly floured surface and gently knead it 2 or 3 times. Pat the dough to ½ inch thick. (I don't roll my biscuit dough; I like to be as gentle with it as possible so the biscuits will not be tough.) Using a 2-inch round biscuit cutter, cut biscuits out of the dough as close together as possible. Transfer the cut biscuits, with sides touching, to the prepared baking sheet. Pat the dough scraps together and cut out the remaining biscuits.

Using the tines of a fork, pierce the top of each biscuit two or three times and brush with the butter. Bake for 12 minutes, or until they are golden brown. Serve immediately.

Clementine Prosecco Marmalade

yields 1 pint

10 small clementines

Granulated sugar

½ cup prosecco

Cut 8 of the clementines into very thin slices and set aside. Squeeze the remaining 2 to make ¼ cup juice; set aside.

Put the clementine slices in a large nonreactive pot, cover with cold water, and bring to a boil over high heat. Lower the heat and simmer for 10 minutes. Drain the water and repeat the process. Drain and let the clementine slices cool.

In a food processor fitted with a metal blade, pulse the clementine slices a few times. (I like my marmalade chunky, but you can continue to pulse if you like yours a bit smoother.) Using a kitchen scale, weigh the cooked clementines. In a large nonreactive pot, combine the clementines and an equal amount of sugar by weight. Stir in the clementine juice and prosecco. Bring to a boil and boil for 10 to 15 minutes, until the marmalade reaches the gel point of 220°F.

Remove from the heat and skim off any foam. Ladle the marmalade into a clean 1-pint canning jar. Let it cool for 10 minutes, then cover and refrigerate until ready to use. Clementine Prosecco Marmalade will keep, refrigerated, for 2 months.

If you don't have a thermometer, you can test to see if the marmalade has set by placing a plate in the freezer when you start cutting the clementines. A few minutes into the final stage of boiling them with the sugar, remove the plate from the freezer and put a small dot of marmalade on the cold plate. Run your finger through the marmalade. If the mixture leaves a clean path on the plate where you ran your finger through and doesn't come back together, your marmalade is done. If it does run back together, keep cooking and retesting again until it sets properly.

Unbaked, cut biscuits can be frozen (lay flat in one layer) in a zip-top bag for up to 30 days. Thaw and bake as directed.

Serrano Ham Croquetas

deep-fried in spanish olive oil : appetizer : serves 6 as tapas

The first time you visit Spain you'll certainly be tasting croquetas similar to these. You will probably have them as one of many tapas options on the table your first day before lunch. Then you'll think about them all day. Have more the next day and the next day and, if like me, every day until you leave. I can't re-create the lively social scene of a fashionable tapas bar in Madrid for you, but I can come pretty close to the flavor on that small plate with this recipe.

¼ cup Spanish extra-virgin olive oil (I use Romanico), plus more for frying

2 shallots, minced

¼ cup all-purpose flour

1 cup milk

¼ teaspoon Spanish paprika

Kosher salt

Freshly ground black pepper

8 ounces serrano ham, finely diced

2 tablespoons minced fresh parsley

2 large eggs

2 cups plain bread crumbs

Simple Sunday Sauce (page 114)

Heat the ¼ cup oil in a medium sauté pan over medium heat. Stir in the shallots and sauté for 5 minutes, or until translucent. Whisk in the flour and cook, whisking, for 2 minutes. Whisk in the milk and cook, whisking, for 8 to 10 minutes, until the sauce thickens. Stir in the paprika. Salt and pepper to taste. Remove the pan from the heat and stir in the ham and parsley. Spoon the mixture into a dish and refrigerate for 1 hour, or until it sets.

Line a baking sheet with paper towels and set aside.

In a wok, heat 4 inches of oil to 360°F. (You can use a deep-fryer, but I like to use my wok for this recipe. Frying in olive oil is essential to achieve the proper flavor of this traditional Spanish recipe.)

In a shallow mixing bowl, beat the eggs together with 2 tablespoons water. Put the bread crumbs in a second shallow mixing bowl. Moisten your hands with water and form the chilled ham mixture into 12 equal-sized balls. Dip each ball first in the bread crumbs, then in the beaten egg, then again in the bread crumbs. Using a slotted metal spoon, gently slip the croquetas, a few at a time, into the hot oil and fry for 1 to 4 minutes, or until golden brown. Serve with the Simple Sunday Sauce for dipping.

Red-Hot Summer Berry Glazed Ham

entrée | serves 10

I prefer to cook a spiral-sliced ham standing on its side, with no tightly wrapped foil restrictions. As the ham cooks, it opens into the most beautiful ruffles of meat. Not only is it magnificent to look at, the waves created by the fanning ham allow the sweet glaze to drip between the layers directly to the bone, crisping up the edges of each slice along its route.

1 (8-pound) Smithfield Spiral Sliced Ham, removed from package, liquid reserved

½ cup seedless raspberry jam

1 cup cranberry juice

½ cup strawberries, roughly chopped, plus more for garnish

½ cup raspberries, plus more for garnish

½ cup honey

1 chipotle chile in adobo sauce, chopped

½ cup dried cranberries

Preheat the oven to 325°F.

In a large roasting pan, place the ham on its side, spiral slices on top.

In a small mixing bowl, whisk together the jam, ½ cup of the cranberry juice, and the reserved liquid from the ham packaging. Pour half of this mixture evenly over the ham; reserve the rest for basting. Cover the roasting pan completely, but very loosely, with aluminum foil (it's important that the foil does not hold the ham slices in place) and bake for 10 minutes per pound (1 hour and 20 minutes for an 8-pound ham), basting the ham occasionally with the reserved jam mixture.

Meanwhile, in a medium saucepan over medium heat, bring the strawberries, raspberries, honey, chipotle, the remaining cranberry juice, and dried cranberries to a simmer. Simmer, stirring occasionally, for 15 minutes, or until the glaze is thick and syrupy.

Increase the oven temperature to 375°F. Remove the foil from the ham and brush the glaze over the top and sides of the ham. Bake for 10 minutes. Remove the ham from the oven and let it rest for 10 minutes before serving. Garnish with fresh berries.

SERRANO HAM

Hedonistic Pig Pizza

pizza sauce · entrée · yields 2 pizzas

Yes, this pizza delivers. No, you can't get this pizza delivered.

3 tablespoons olive oil

1 packet active dry yeast

2 teaspoons sugar

1 teaspoon kosher salt

4 cups all-purpose flour

Cornmeal for dusting the pan

Pizza Sauce (recipe follows)

2½ cups grated mozzarella cheese

6 slices serrano ham

4 ounces pepperoni, thinly sliced

8 ounces Italian sausage, casings removed, chopped and fully cooked

1 cup freshly grated Parmesan cheese

Preheat the oven to 450°F. Using 1 tablespoon of the oil, grease the insides of two medium mixing bowls. Set aside.

In the bowl of a stand mixer fitted with a dough hook, combine 1 cup warm water with the yeast, sugar, and remaining oil. Let sit for 5 minutes for the yeast mixture to bloom. Add the salt and stir until combined. Add the flour and stir until the dough begins to form a ball and pull away from the sides of the bowl. Turn the dough out onto a lightly floured surface and knead it for 6 to 8 minutes. Divide the dough in half and place one piece in each of the greased bowls. Cover the bowls and set aside in a warm place to rise until the dough doubles in size, about 1 hour. Using your hands, punch down both doughs and knead again for 4 minutes. Return the dough balls to the greased bowls and let the dough rise for 20 minutes.

After the dough has risen again, remove one dough ball at a time to a floured surface and roll it to your desired size and thickness. Place rolled dough on an overturned preheated baking sheet or pizza pan that has been dusted with cornmeal. Bake for 5 minutes. Remove from the oven and top each pizza with 1 cup Pizza Sauce and 1 cup of mozzarella cheese. Divide the ham, pepperoni, and sausage between the two pizzas and top each with the remaining mozzarella and the Parmesan.

Bake the pizzas one at a time for 10 minutes or more, until the crust has browned and the cheese is bubbly.

Pizza Sauce

yields 4 cups

2 tablespoons olive oil

1 small yellow onion, finely diced

2 cloves garlic, minced

2 teaspoons dried oregano

1 teaspoon kosher salt

¼ teaspoon red pepper flakes

Pinch of sugar

1 (28-ounce) can crushed San Marzano tomatoes

4 ounces tomato paste

1 bay leaf

Heat the oil in a medium saucepan over medium heat, then stir in the onion, garlic, oregano, salt, and red pepper flakes. Sauté for 5 minutes, until the onion is translucent. Stir in the remaining ingredients and bring to a boil. Lower the heat and simmer, uncovered, for 1 hour. Remove the bay leaf before saucing the pizzas. Leftover pizza sauce can be stored in the refrigerator for 7 days, or in the freezer for 3 months.

7

Offal

jowl : head : feet : ears : fatback : clear plate : tail

organ meats (intestines, stomach, skin, liver)

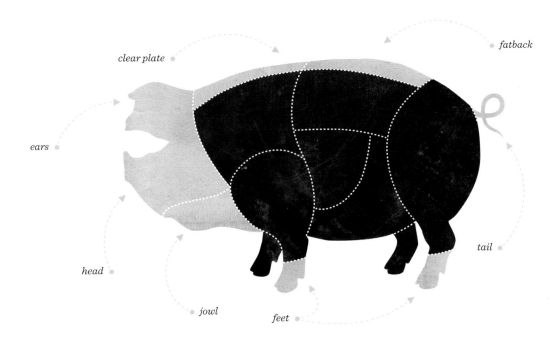

fatback

clear plate

ears

head

jowl

feet

tail

Offal is practically a whole class of food in itself. The term literally means "off fall," or the pieces which fall from a carcass when it is butchered. At one time, it principally applied to the entrails. In the USA, we currently use the terms "organ meats" or "variety meats" to cover all the abdominal organs and extremities like the heart, liver, lungs (usually called the pluck), tails, head, brain, tongue, and feet. Offal includes cuts like the jowl, which is the fat cut of meat along the side of the head—basically, the cheek area, usually cured to make Italian guanciale. And the feet, the area on the pig from the ankles to the toes. In this chapter, I cover every cut I use that cannot be confined to the other chapters. From chitterlings (intestines) to liver. With offal, the challenge is only in your head. I urge you to give a cut you might not normally consider a try. It's all really tasty, and that's the offal truth. (Sorry, I had to.)

Cooking Methods: A variety of cooking techniques are used for this cross section of "extras." Jowls are cured. Heads are braised. Feet are cured, smoked, or pickled. Skin is fried. Liver is sautéed. It really just depends on the cut and your creativity.

Classic Spaghetti alla Carbonara

For one year I sailed with my husband and son aboard our own sailboat. I learned to make this spaghetti alla carbonara in the most unexpected way. Our boat was one of only two anchored off a leeward beach on the island of Barbuda, so it made sense that I would be friendly toward the owners of the other boat when we crossed paths onshore. That's how I met Patricia. She was a hard Roman woman—her eyebrows set in a permanent scowl as if the sun were perpetually stinging her eyes. Her English was pretty much nonexistent, but my culinary Italian was just good enough to discern that she was making spaghetti alla carbonara and—surprisingly—that we were invited for dinner! Patricia might not have been the queen of warm welcomes, but I wasn't going to turn down an Italian meal from a Roman woman. Going aboard Patricia's boat was like stepping onto a floating butcher shop filled with screaming Italians. There may have been only three people there, but it sounded like a World Cup soccer match was being played onboard. Patricia greeted me (relatively speaking) barefoot, wielding an excessively large knife in her hand and with a glare in her eye (the image still haunts me to this day).

I obediently followed her to the starboard guest cabin, which was cooled and entirely full of hanging meat in various stages of processing and drying. Just as I thought I was at my final resting place, she directed me over to the guanciale and expertly cut off six thin slices. She paused a moment to scream at somebody in the next cabin, and then she walked me over to an enormous cloth-covered round of Parmesan, where, using the same knife, she cut off a large chunk. Twenty minutes and several rounds of screaming later, we sat down to the best Italian dinner I've ever had. I still think of Patricia each time I make this carbonara; I wonder where she is, if she's still living on a boat, still curing and drying her own meats, and if she's used that knife to kill anyone yet.

Classic Spaghetti alla Carbonara (page 152)

Classic Spaghetti alla Carbonara

entrée   serves 4

Kosher salt

3 tablespoons olive oil

**8 ounces guanciale, thinly sliced;
or pancetta, cut into small pieces**

2 teaspoons freshly ground black pepper,
or more to taste

1 pound dried spaghetti

1½ cups finely grated Parmesan cheese,
plus more for garnish

4 large eggs, at room temperature

In a large pot, bring 6 quarts salted water to a rolling boil.

In a large skillet, heat the oil. Stir in the guanciale and cook, stirring occasionally, for 6 minutes, or until lightly browned. Stir in the pepper and cook for 2 minutes. Remove from the heat and transfer the contents of the skillet to a large mixing bowl. Let cool slightly.

Add the spaghetti to the boiling water and cook for 8 to 10 minutes, or until it is al dente. Drain the pasta, reserving 1 cup of the pasta water.

Add the cheese and eggs to the slightly cooled guanciale. Using a wooden spoon, vigorously stir the mixture until the sauce thickens to the consistency of mayonnaise. Transfer the cooked pasta (still hot) to the bowl and toss it with the guanciale sauce. Add the reserved pasta water, a little at a time, until the sauce coats the pasta and becomes creamy (you probably won't need all of the water). Salt and pepper to taste. Serve immediately, garnished with more Parmesan cheese.

Guanciale is made by rubbing spices into the meat from a hog's jowls and drying it. From start to finish, guanciale takes at least 4 weeks, but the wait is worth it.

Sweet Apple Scrapple

....

fried eggs, maple syrup   entrée   serves 6

....

The perfect farmyard breakfast food.

8 ounces pork liver or beef liver

6 cups pork stock (page 154) or beef stock

1 pound ground pork

1 Granny Smith apple, peeled, cored, and finely diced

1 tablespoon Grade A maple syrup, plus more for serving

1½ cups cornmeal

½ cup buckwheat flour

½ teaspoon ground dried sage

1 teaspoon dried marjoram

¼ teaspoon ground allspice

2 tablespoons kosher salt

2 teaspoons freshly ground black pepper

2 tablespoons bacon fat

¼ cup self-rising flour

6 eggs, poached or fried

Line a 9-by-5-by-3-inch loaf pan with plastic wrap, allowing the edges of the wrap to hang over by 3 inches on all sides. Set aside.

Put the liver in a large pot and cover with the stock. Place over medium heat and simmer for 10 minutes. Remove the liver from the stock and roughly chop. Return the chopped liver to the simmering stock and stir in the ground pork. Simmer for 15 minutes, then stir in the apple and maple syrup.

In a large mixing bowl, whisk together the cornmeal, buckwheat flour, sage, marjoram, allspice, salt, and pepper. Slowly whisk the cornmeal mixture into the simmering stock. Simmer for 1 hour, stirring often. The mixture will be very thick. Spoon the mixture into the prepared loaf pan, smooth the top, and tap it down. Fold the edges of the plastic wrap over to cover. Let cool to room temperature, then refrigerate overnight.

Heat the bacon fat in a large skillet over medium heat. Unwrap the scrapple loaf and cut it into ½-inch slices. Dredge the slices in the self-rising flour, and fry in bacon fat until browned and crisp on both sides. Remove the fried scrapple to a serving platter and top each slice with a poached or fried egg. Drizzle with maple syrup and serve.

Have scrapple left over? Try a scrapple panini. Spread two slices of pumpernickel bread with prepared apple butter. Place a slice of fried scrapple on one piece of bread; add a thick slice of swiss cheese and a few thin slices of tart apple. Top with the other bread slice. Grill the sandwich in a panini press until toasted and cheese has melted.

Pork Stock

yields 4 quarts

In French cooking, stocks are called *fonds de cuisine,* literally the "foundations of cooking." I'm not French (although I do kiss that way), but I worship this same god. Homemade stocks supply richness, texture, and layers of flavor to every dish. The last time I used a store-bought stock, Clinton was in the White House.

4 pounds uncooked pork bones (neck, hock, steak, or roast bones)

2 large carrots, roughly chopped

2 large onions, unpeeled, halved

2 scallions, roughly chopped

4 celery hearts, roughly chopped

2 cloves garlic, smashed

1 slice fresh ginger

10 black peppercorns

2 sprigs fresh thyme

2 bay leaves

1 teaspoon kosher salt

Preheat the oven to 400°F.

In a large roasting pan, arrange the pork bones in a single layer and roast for 30 minutes, flipping as necessary, until they turn golden brown. Remove the bones to a plate and set aside. Reserve 2 tablespoons fat from the roasting pan and set aside. Discard any remaining fat. Place the roasting pan over medium-high heat and add 1 cup water to deglaze the pan, scraping up all the brown bits from the bottom and sides of the pan. Set aside.

In a large stockpot over high heat, heat the reserved fat. Stir in the carrots, onions, scallions, celery, garlic, and ginger. Sauté for 10 minutes, or until the onions begin to brown. To the sautéed vegetables, add the liquid from the roasting pan, the bones, peppercorns, thyme, bay leaves, salt, and enough cold water to cover. Bring to a boil, then lower the heat and simmer, uncovered, for 6 hours. Skim off any foam that forms on the surface as the stock cooks.

Strain the stock and discard any solids. The stock may be stored in the refrigerator for up to 2 weeks, or frozen for up to 1 year.

Stockpile hock bones and any bones removed from roasts and steaks in a plastic bag in the freezer until you have enough to make a stock.

clockwise from top left:
Pork Stock,
Snack Cracklin's (page 156),
Old No. 7 Pâté (page 160),
Chitterlings (page 157)

Snack Cracklin's

double-fried ∴ appetizer ∴ serves 6

1 pound pork skin

2 teaspoons kosher salt, plus more for sprinkling

Peanut oil for frying

Preheat the oven to 375°F. Line a baking sheet with paper towels and set aside.

Using a sharp knife, score one side of the pork skin without cutting all the way through. Rub the 2 teaspoons salt into both sides of the skin. Put the skin in a roasting pan and roast for 10 to 15 minutes, until the fat has rendered and the skin is light golden and crisp. Remove from the oven and transfer the cracklings to the prepared baking sheet to drain until they are cool enough to handle.

In a deep-fryer or Dutch oven, heat 2 inches oil to 360°F.

Remove the cracklings to a cutting board and put a fresh layer of paper towels on the baking sheet. Chop the roasted cracklings up into small snack-size pieces (the size of a large cashew). Fry the cracklings for 2 to 3 minutes, until dark golden. Remove and drain on the prepared baking sheet. Sprinkle lightly with salt while hot. Eat while still warm or allow to cool and store in an airtight container for up to 2 weeks.

For extra flavor on your Snack Cracklin's, make your own finishing salts to sprinkle over the just-fried cracklings. A simple finishing salt ratio is ¼ cup salt (I use kosher) stirred together with 1 teaspoon of the spice of your choice.

Chitterlings

serves 10

I was told there are two important rules about cooking chitterlings (chitlins):
(1) If they stink when you get them, they are fresh. (2) If they stink (too much) while cooking them,
you didn't clean them well enough. I learned both rules the hard way.

20 pounds chitterlings

6 large baking potatoes, peeled

Kosher salt

2 large onions, peeled and halved

1 green bell pepper, chopped

3 cloves garlic, peeled and smashed

2 jalapeño chiles, cut in half

3 ribs celery, with leaves

1 cup cider vinegar

1 bay leaf

Louisiana hot sauce (lots of it!)

Cleaning your chitterlings properly takes patience. Bring a large stockpot of water to a boil. Add the chitterlings and 2 potatoes (the potatoes will help eliminate some of the odor when cooking) and parboil them for 5 minutes. Remove from the heat and let the chitterlings cool enough to handle. Discard the potatoes and water, and thoroughly clean the pot before using again.

Using your fingers, separate the membrane—a thin, clear piece of fat—from the chitterlings. Continue the cleaning process using two pots and one sink, with the tap water running: Put the chitterlings in one pot and cover with water to soak until you start cleaning them. One by one, clean each chitterling by running it under the tap water and removing all the fat, undigested food, and any specks that you see. Once cleaned, put the chitterling in a second pot filled with clean, salted water. Repeat this process at least five times, until the water in the second pot is no longer cloudy and greasy. If some areas are difficult to clean, cut the chitterling with a knife to open and clean the dirty area. When chitterlings are clean, they will look slightly transparent.

In a large stockpot, put the cleaned chitterlings and 2 more potatoes. Cover with water, bring to a boil, and boil for 5 minutes. Skim off any fat, remove the chitterlings, discard the potatoes, and thoroughly clean the pot. Return the chitterlings to the cleaned stockpot and add just enough water to come three-quarters up the sides. Bring the water to a rolling boil and add the remaining 2 potatoes, 2 tablespoons salt, the onions, bell pepper, garlic, jalapeños, celery, vinegar, and bay leaf. Lower the heat to medium-low and simmer for 3 to 4 hours, until desired tenderness is achieved. Continue to skim off the fat during the cooking process.

Remove the chitterlings from the cooking liquid and discard the vegetables and bay leaf. Pour off all but 2 cups of the cooking liquid. Cut the chitterlings into pieces and return them to the pot with the reserved cooking liquid. Cook to heat through. Drain and serve with lots of hot sauce.

Chitterlings, like collard greens, cook way down. Twenty pounds of chitterlings will cook down to about ten pounds.

Once thoroughly cooked, chitterlings can be cut into bite-size pieces, dipped in beaten egg, rolled in fine saltine cracker crumbs, and deep-fried in 360°F peanut oil until golden brown.

how to

Tough to pronounce. Easy to prepare. Best to partake.

6 trotters (pig's feet from the hind legs)

6 cups distilled white vinegar

2 jalapeño chiles

3 serrano chiles

1 medium sweet onion, thinly sliced

6 slices fresh ginger

1 tablespoon coriander seeds

2 teaspoons mustard seeds

4 black peppercorns

4 bay leaves

2 tablespoons kosher salt

1 Prepare the pig's feet by burning off any visible hair. To do this, hold one at a time over a gas flame on the stovetop or use a kitchen torch, then rinse with cold water until thoroughly clean. Sterilize one 2-quart glass jar with a lid, or two 1-quart canning jars.

2 Using a cleaver, split the pig's feet in half lengthwise.

3 Put the split pig's feet in a large pot and cover with water.

4 Bring the water to a boil, lower the heat to low, and simmer, stirring occasionally, for 1½ to 2 hours, until the pig's feet are tender. While the pig's feet are cooking, skim off any foam from the surface.

5 Remove the feet from the cooking liquid, rinse with water, and set them aside. Discard the cooking liquid and clean the pot thoroughly.

6 Combine the vinegar, chiles, onion, ginger, remaining spices, the bay leaves, and salt in the clean pot and bring to a boil. Lower the heat to low and simmer for 10 minutes.

7 Add the cooked, cooled pig's feet to the vinegar mixture and bring to a boil. Remove from the heat and let cool slightly.

8 Transfer the pig's feet to the sterilized jar(s), layering them with the chiles, onion, and spices. Pour in enough pickling liquid to cover, then cover and refrigerate. Partake of Hot Peppered Pickled Pig's Feet within 7 days after preparation.

A pig's foot a day could keep the wrinkles away . . . say practitioners of superfood eating. You see, pig's feet contain high amounts of the protein collagen. Collagen works hand in hand with keratin to provide the skin with strength and resilience and is often referred to as the glue that holds the body together. Armed with this knowledge, I'm counting on my love of pig's feet to help forty be the new thirty.

Old No. 7 Pâté

tipsy pork liver   appetizer   yields 3 cups

Liver is a funny thing. You either love it or hate it. My friend Jamie flips for my liver pâté. To him, it's the meat-and-butter version of honey—all rich, silky, and spreadable. Maybe he was born with an affinity for it; after all, his mother, Rita, claims that she craved liver so much during her pregnancy that she hates the sight of it now. She swoons at the mere mention of it, employing all the drama of Ann Darrow from *King Kong*—complete with hand to the forehead. (It's an Oscar-worthy performance, but a bit much for a dinner party.) Knowing this, I wouldn't risk bringing a jar over to Jamie's house if I thought his mother would be around. I just can't bear the histrionics. However, at a recent potluck appetizer party that I knew Jamie would also be attending, I couldn't resist bringing him two jars of my Old No. 7 Pâté. Jamie brought Rita. Let's just say you would've thought I'd unleashed a sixty-ton primate.

1 cup (2 sticks) unsalted butter

½ cup plus 1 tablespoon finely diced sweet onion

1 large clove garlic, minced

1 teaspoon minced fresh thyme, or ¼ teaspoon dried

1 teaspoon minced fresh marjoram, or ¼ teaspoon dried

1 teaspoon minced fresh sage, or ¼ teaspoon dried, plus whole fresh sage leaves for garnish

¾ teaspoon kosher salt

¼ teaspoon ground allspice

Pinch of freshly ground black pepper

8 ounces pork liver, trimmed

8 ounces chicken livers, trimmed

2 tablespoons Old No. 7 Tennessee Whiskey

Crackers or French bread

In a large nonstick sauté pan, melt 1 stick of the butter. Add the onion and garlic and cook until they have softened. Add the thyme, marjoram, minced sage, salt, allspice, pepper, and pork and chicken livers. Cook, stirring, for 6 to 8 minutes, until the livers are cooked on the outside but still pink on the inside. Stir in the whiskey and remove from the heat. Pour the pork liver mixture into a food processor fitted with a metal blade and process until just smooth. Pour into a sterilized glass jar or jars.

Clarify the remaining butter: Melt the butter in a small saucepan over low heat. Remove from the heat and let stand for 5 minutes. Skim the froth from the top of the melted butter and pour the clear butter into a bowl or cup. Discard the milky solids left in the bottom of the pan.

Place 1 sage leaf on top of the smoothed pâté in each jar and spoon enough clarified butter over the pâté to cover the surface. Put the pâté in the refrigerator, uncovered, until it sets; then cover tightly, return the jar to the refrigerator, and chill for at least 2 hours. Serve with crackers or bread. (This is also great atop grilled beef.)

Old No. 7 Pork Liver Pâté can be refrigerated for 2 weeks without the butter seal broken, and 1 week after the seal has been broken.

Hangover Irish Crubeens

shandy style | appetizer | serves 2

Who said you can't eat feet with your fingers? After all, if you're enjoying this hangover feast, having proper table manners is the least of your worries.

6 trotters (pig's feet from the hind legs), cleaned (see step 1 on page 158)

1 large sweet onion, quartered

2 carrots, peeled

2 sprigs fresh thyme

1 bay leaf

4 whole cloves

8 black peppercorns

½ bunch fresh parsley

1 cup prepared fresh lemonade

1 (12-ounce) bottle Smithwick's Ale, or your favorite ale

In a large Dutch oven, combine all the ingredients. Pour in just enough cold water to barely cover the trotters and bring to a boil. Skim the surface of any fat and foam. Lower the heat, cover, and simmer for 3 hours, or until the meat is tender. Remove the pig's feet from the pot and serve warm or cold. Eat these using your fingers!

8

Slices

leaf lard ⦙ sliced bacon

slices

From subtle to icky gooey, this chapter is about shameless sweets. The one ingredient that a lot of these recipes have in common is leaf fat, and it will change your life. Leaf fat is harvested from around the kidneys, inside the loin. I'll show you how to render it down to lard and use it to make blue-ribbon-winning pies and tarts with the flakiest crusts. Sliced bacon is a welcome complement to many of the inventive chocolate desserts in this chapter. To me, bacon and chocolate are like short skirts and ballet flats. They just go well together.

Cooking Methods: Leaf lard is made by slowly rendering leaf fat. In this chapter, bacon is always pan-fried.

Annie Mae's Popcorn Balls

My grandmother on my father's side, Annie Mae, lived just a twenty-minute drive from my hog-farming grandma, Lula Mae, but the only thing they had in common was Mae. You see, Annie Mae lived "in town." She drove a car with a peeling "I'm a Democrat" sticker on the back, was a devout Southern Baptist and the first in her family to go to college . . . but she'd never earn a passing grade in what the ladies of her day would call home economics. The doilies on her living room furniture might have been in just the right place, but you could write your name in the thick layer of dust surrounding them. When she passed away a few years ago, it was a coin flip as to who would have to clean her kitchen. I didn't care too much about her domestic limitations. What I loved about Annie Mae—aside from her sweet tooth—was her jewelry. She had a copious collection of cocktail jewelry that she would put in a large box for my sisters and me to play with when we came over to visit. Long after my sisters grew bored, I'd still be sitting there adorned with jewelry, imagining which pieces I would wear for my next guest spot on *The Mike Douglas Show.*

Around Christmastime, it's customary that even noncooks get motivated to try their hand at the art of cooking. Annie Mae was no exception. She would make batches of Martha Washington candy that I would liken to chocolate-flavored coconut wax lips. Peanut brittle you could pave a street with. Sugar cookies that even Santa would leave behind. But the one thing she did better than anyone, then or since, was molasses popcorn balls. I would eat three before dinner, two after dinner, and squirrel away as many others as I could while the family was distracted by a dance number on *The Lawrence Welk Show.* For a fall party a couple of years ago, I made Grandmother Annie Mae's molasses popcorn balls studded with candied bacon. The guests are still asking me for the recipe. I'm happy to share it with you now. Most of all, I'm happy to have had Annie Mae in my life, and I'm honored to wear some of the fabulous jewelry (now vintage) she left me when I make these popcorn balls. I love you, Grandma.

Annie Mae's Popcorn Balls (page 166)

Annie Mae's Popcorn Balls

sweet molasses and bacon | dessert | yields 18 to 20

12 cups warm cooked popcorn

1½ cups sugar

⅔ cup molasses

Pinch of kosher salt

½ teaspoon vinegar

⅓ cup unsalted butter, plus more to grease baking sheet and hands

1 tablespoon vanilla extract

8 slices bacon, cooked crisp, diced

Grease a baking sheet with butter and set aside.

Put the popcorn in a large roasting pan and keep it warm while you make the molasses bacon coating.

In a heavy saucepan over medium-low heat, stir together the sugar, molasses, 1 cup water, the salt, and vinegar. Cook, stirring constantly, until the mixture begins to boil and reaches 250°F when tested with a candy thermometer (this is the hard ball stage). Remove from the heat and stir in the butter, vanilla, and bacon. Slowly pour the mixture over the warm popcorn and mix well, using a wooden spoon. When the popcorn has cooled just enough to handle, butter your hands well and make baseball-sized balls by pressing the mixture together firmly, but gently enough not to crush the popcorn.

Put the warm popcorn balls onto the buttered baking sheet and let them cool until they have hardened. To store, wrap them individually in plastic wrap. Popcorn balls will keep for 5 to 7 days unrefrigerated.

For an unexpected parting gift for your best girlfriends, wrap individual popcorn balls in plastic wrap and secure with a beautiful ribbon aglitter with a piece of vintage jewelry. I guarantee the plastic wrap will come off before the car's out of the driveway.

Way Better Than Basic Pie Dough

leaf lard, butter, vanilla sugar	yields enough for 1 double-crust pie

Stop right now and clear a space for your blue ribbons. My Way Better Than Basic Pie Dough makes the most flavorful and flaky crust you have ever eaten. This recipe will change your life.

2½ cups all-purpose flour

½ teaspoon kosher salt

1 tablespoon Vanilla Sugar (recipe follows)

12 tablespoons cold unsalted butter, cubed

¼ cup cold rendered leaf lard (page 170) or vegetable shortening

¼ to ½ cup ice water

In a large mixing bowl, whisk together the flour, salt, and Vanilla Sugar. Using two forks or a pastry blender, cut in the butter and lard, making sure to leave some chunks of butter the size of peas. Stir the ice water into the flour mixture until a ball has formed. Work quickly and do not overmix. Form the mixture into two equal-sized disks. Cover with plastic wrap and chill in the refrigerator for 2 hours. The dough will be a little crumbly.

The dough can be refrigerated for up to 2 days or frozen for up to 3 months.

Vanilla Sugar

yields 2 cups

1 organic vanilla bean

2 cups sugar

Using a sharp paring knife, cut a slit down the side of the organic vanilla bean, remove the seeds, and place them, along with the bean, in a 1-quart jar with a lid. Fill the jar with the sugar. Screw on the lid and give it a good shake. Let the sugar sit in a cool pantry for 2 weeks to attain peak flavor before using (although I've been known to use it after just 2 days). Keep adding more sugar to the jar as you use it. One vanilla bean will last through three jars of sugar.

SLICED BACON

Bacon Banana Cookies

anthony's favorite | dessert | yields 30 cookies

Ginger, my mother, never liked a bunch of kids in her house. Even as a young girl, I could feel her angst when too many neighborhood kids were around. Her clever solution was to bake a plate of my favorite Bacon Banana Cookies and leave them on the front porch, locking the door behind her. I never minded being sequestered outside with my food loot in the summer because the porch concrete cooled my skin. The winter—that was a different story.

When I bake these cookies now for my son, Anthony, I'm secretly baking them for myself. I wonder if my mom did the same thing? I'll be sure to ask her . . . as soon as she unlocks the front door.

2½ cups sifted all-purpose flour

2 teaspoons baking powder

¼ teaspoon baking soda

1½ teaspoons ground cinnamon

¼ teaspoon kosher salt

½ cup (1 stick) unsalted butter

1¼ cups sugar

2 large eggs

1 teaspoon vanilla extract

4 bananas, mashed (about 1⅓ cups)

½ pound bacon, cooked crisp, chopped

Preheat the oven to 400°F. Line a baking sheet with parchment paper and set aside.

In a large mixing bowl, sift together the flour, baking powder, baking soda, ½ teaspoon of the cinnamon, and the salt.

In a medium mixing bowl, use a hand mixer to cream together the butter and 1 cup of the sugar. Beat in the eggs, one at a time, until they are fully incorporated. Beat in the vanilla. Add the butter mixture to the flour mixture, then stir in the mashed bananas, beating well after each addition. Fold in the bacon.

Stir together the remaining ¼ cup sugar and the remaining cinnamon. Set aside.

Drop the dough by heaping tablespoons onto the prepared baking sheet 1 inch apart. Sprinkle generously with the cinnamon-sugar and bake for 10 to 12 minutes, until slightly browned. Allow the cookies to cool completely before storing in an airtight container. Cookies will keep for 5 to 7 days.

Rock-hard bananas? Ripen them quickly for Bacon Banana Cookies by placing the peeled fruit on a parchment-lined baking sheet and cooking them in a 400°F oven for 10 minutes until they are soft.

Next time you make banana bread, try stirring 4 slices cooked and chopped bacon into the batter.

how to

Render Leaf Lard | yields 2 quarts

If you think back to the best pie you've ever had, with the flakiest crust, there's a good possibility the crust was made from leaf lard. Leaf lard is the highest grade of lard and is obtained from the fat deposit around the kidneys and inside the loin of a pig. It's ideal for use in baked goods as it has little or no pork flavor, and it is the well-kept secret of pastry chefs around the world, but no secret to country cooks like my grandmother Lula Mae. Grandma made pies with the flakiest crusts, and because she dabbled in hog farming, I can only presume her secret was leaf lard. I carry on her tradition of pie-making pride with my own special mixture of leaf lard and butter crust pies. Follow these simple step-by-step instructions for rendering leaf lard, and you will undoubtedly realize how simple the process is—and will want to keep a quart in your refrigerator or freezer at all times. Ask your butcher about purchasing leaf fat. You may need to source it directly from a local hog farmer in your area. Check the Source Guide (page 186) for farmers in your region.

5 pounds pork leaf fat, chopped

Dutch oven

Wooden spoon

Fine-mesh strainer

2 (1-quart) clean canning jars, bands, and lids

1 Roughly chop the fat.

2 Heat a Dutch oven over medium-low heat. Add the fat and 1 cup water.

3 Cook, stirring every 15 minutes with a wooden spoon, for 1 hour, or until the fat begins to melt.

4 When the fat melts further, you'll hear a few loud pops. This is the last of the air and moisture leaving what will soon be the cracklings (fried pieces of pork, typically a thick layer of fat and small bits of meat). When you hear these pops, begin stirring more frequently for the next 15 minutes.

5 Strain and remove the cracklings that float to the surface.

6 When the remaining cracklings sink to the bottom of the pan, the lard has been fully rendered and the liquid will be yellow. Remove from the heat and let the lard cool slightly.

7 Pour the lard through a fine strainer into sterilized canning jars. Save the cracklings left in the bottom of the pan for a snack!

8 Refrigerate the jar of lard overnight, uncovered. The lard will solidify and turn white. Replace the lid, cover tightly, and store the lard in the refrigerator for up to 4 months or in the freezer for 1 year.

1 pound of leaf fat
renders about
1 pint leaf lard

Best Ever Family Reunion Chocolate Sheet Cake

bacon pecan icing · dessert · serves 20

The only thing I recognized at the last family reunion I attended was this amazing cake. It had been ten years since I tasted it the last time and, unlike everything and everyone around me, it was still decadently the same. Same size, same marital status, same job . . . just its same perfect self. I decided to make it better.

2 cups all-purpose flour

2 cups sugar

1 teaspoon baking soda

¼ teaspoon ground cinnamon

¼ teaspoon kosher salt

¾ cup (1½ sticks) unsalted butter

¼ cup leaf lard (page 170) or vegetable shortening

¼ cup good-quality cocoa powder

2 large eggs, beaten

½ cup buttermilk

1 teaspoon vanilla extract

Bacon Pecan Icing (recipe follows)

Preheat the oven to 350°F. Grease a 15½-by-10½-by-2-inch baking pan and set aside.

In a large mixing bowl, whisk together the flour, sugar, baking soda, cinnamon, and salt.

In a medium saucepan over medium heat, melt the butter and lard. Bring 1 cup water to a boil in a separate small pan. Whisk the cocoa powder and boiling water into the butter mixture. Boil for 30 seconds, then remove from the heat and pour the mixture over the dry ingredients. Stir until just combined.

In a small mixing bowl, whisk together the eggs, buttermilk, and vanilla. Add to the cocoa mixture and whisk until fully incorporated. Pour into the prepared baking pan and bake for 15 minutes, or until set. Frost the cake while it's still warm. Let the frosting set up for 10 minutes before serving. Serve warm or at room temperature.

Bacon Pecan Icing

yields 3¼ cups

14 tablespoons (1¾ sticks) unsalted butter, at room temperature

¼ cup good-quality cocoa powder

½ cup buttermilk

1 teaspoon vanilla extract

3½ cups confectioners' sugar, sifted

1 cup pecans, toasted and coarsely chopped

4 slices Smithfield  bacon, cooked crisp, finely diced

Put the butter, cocoa powder, buttermilk, and vanilla in the bowl of a stand mixer fitted with the whisk attachment and whisk until all ingredients are fully incorporated. Add the confectioners' sugar 1 cup at a time, mixing thoroughly after each addition. Remove the bowl from the mixer and stir in the pecans and bacon.

Mini Tart Tarts

lemons, key limes : dessert : serves 6

¼ cup (½ stick) cold unsalted butter, cut into small pieces

¼ cup cold leaf lard (page 170) or vegetable shortening

¼ cup Vanilla Sugar (page 167)

1 cup all-purpose flour, plus more for dusting

1 teaspoon freshly ground black pepper

¼ teaspoon kosher salt

8 large egg yolks

1 tablespoon grated lemon zest

1 tablespoon grated lime zest, plus more for garnish

½ cup plus 2 tablespoons freshly squeezed lemon juice

½ cup bottled Key lime juice

2 (14-ounce) cans sweetened condensed milk

2 large egg whites

¼ teaspoon cream of tartar

¼ cup superfine sugar

Preheat the oven to 325°F. Grease six 4-inch round fluted tart pans and place on two baking sheets. Set aside.

In the bowl of a stand mixer fitted with the whisk attachment set on medium-low speed, beat the butter, lard, and Vanilla Sugar for 20 seconds, or until just combined. Add the flour, pepper, and ⅛ teaspoon of the salt and beat for 1 minute. Increase the speed to medium-high and beat for 1 to 2 minutes more, until a wet dough forms.

On a lightly floured work surface, divide the dough into 6 equal portions. Press each portion into a tart pan to line it. Bake for 20 minutes, or until the crusts are a pale golden brown. Let cool on the baking sheets. Keep the oven at 325°F while you make the filling.

In a medium mixing bowl, whisk together the egg yolks, lemon and lime zest and juice, sweetened condensed milk, and the remaining ⅛ teaspoon salt. Pour the filling into the tart shells and bake for 12 minutes, or until the filling begins to puff and the edges are firm to the touch. Let cool, then chill in the refrigerator for 1 hour. After 1 hour, remove the sides of the tart pans. Return the tarts to the refrigerator to chill, uncovered, overnight.

In a large mixing bowl with a hand mixer on high speed, beat the egg whites and cream of tartar just until soft peaks form. Gradually beat in the superfine sugar, and continue to beat until the meringue is glossy and forms stiff peaks.

Preheat the broiler.

Remove the bases from the tarts, and return the tarts to one baking sheet. Transfer the meringue to a pastry bag fitted with a large star tip, and pipe a dollop of meringue on top of each tart. Broil for 30 seconds, or until the top of the meringue begins to brown. Serve immediately.

No-Fake Gooey Butter Cake

the original, st. louis style | dessert | serves 18 (makes 2 cakes)

The thing that makes this cake gooey is the barely baked butter filling—when you slice a piece it should slowly ooze onto your plate. Unless you are eating it in St. Louis, Missouri, right now, it's highly likely that piece of Gooey Butter Cake you're reaching for is an imposter. Let me introduce you to the real Midwestern thing—an above-average-looking, hardworking cake, with a good middle-class background, but not too sweet.

1 packet active dry yeast

½ cup warm milk

2¾ cups granulated sugar

¼ cup leaf lard (page 170) or vegetable shortening

¼ teaspoon plus ⅛ teaspoon kosher salt

2 large eggs

4¾ cups all-purpose flour

2 tablespoons vanilla extract

1 cup (2 sticks) unsalted butter, softened

¼ cup light corn syrup

4 tablespoons confectioners' sugar

Gooey Butter Cake is best when served at room temperature, so the butter can ooze! Refrigerate leftovers and allow to come to room temperature before eating.

clockwise from top left:
Ginger's Dark Chocolate Ginger Pie (page 178),
No-Fake Gooey Butter Cake,
Pie Dough Scrap Shortcake (page 179)

In a small bowl, dissolve the yeast in the milk and set aside.

In the bowl of a stand mixer fitted with the whisk attachment, cream ¼ cup of the granulated sugar, the lard, and ¼ teaspoon of the salt until light and fluffy. Add 1 of the eggs and beat well. Change the whisk attachment to a dough hook and add the 2½ cups of flour, yeast mixture, and 1 tablespoon of the vanilla. Mix for 3 minutes. Turn the dough out onto a lightly floured board and knead with your hands for an additional minute.

Lightly grease a bowl and put the dough inside, turning once. Cover the bowl with a towel and set aside in a warm place to rise for 1 hour.

Grease two 8-inch square stoneware baking pans and set aside.

Divide the dough into 2 equal parts. Using your hands, pat the dough into the bottom of each prepared baking dish and up the sides. With a fork, prick the dough in a few places so it doesn't bubble up when baking. Set aside while you prepare the gooey part.

Combine the remaining granulated sugar, the butter, and the remaining salt in the bowl of a stand mixer fitted with a whisk attachment. Mix until very fluffy. Add the remaining egg and the corn syrup, mixing well after each addition. Finally, add the remaining flour, ¼ cup water, and the remaining vanilla, mixing well after each addition. Divide the gooey butter equally between the two prepared pans. Using a spatula, spread the mixture evenly over the dough in each pan. Let the cakes rest for 20 minutes before baking.

Preheat the oven to 375°F. Bake for 20 to 25 minutes, until the tops begin to turn golden brown. Do not overbake. Remove the cakes from the oven and let cool completely on a wire rack. Sprinkle each cake with 2 tablespoons of the confectioners' sugar. Serve at room temperature.

Ginger's Dark Chocolate Ginger Pie

baked meringue | dessert | serves 8

Ginger is my mother. Growing up, none of my friend's mothers had such an "exotic" name. I loved saying her name, and to this day I still refer to her using her full name, Ginger Patrick—not Mom. This is Ginger Patrick's pie. A rich, dark chocolate pie with just a subtle hint of ginger—not at all like Ginger Patrick.

½ recipe Way Better Than Basic Pie Dough, for single-crust pie (page 167)

1 cup Vanilla Sugar (page 167) or regular sugar plus 1 teaspoon vanilla extract

1 cup evaporated milk

3 heaping tablespoons cornstarch

3 tablespoons good-quality dark cocoa powder

¼ teaspoon ground ginger

4 large egg yolks, beaten

2½ tablespoons unsalted butter, softened

6 large egg whites

½ teaspoon cream of tartar

⅓ cup superfine sugar

Preheat the oven to 425°F.

On a lightly floured surface, roll out the dough round into a 12-inch circle and drape it into a 9-inch pie plate, leaving a 1-inch overhang. Take care not to stretch the dough. Decoratively crimp the edges. Blind bake (or prebake) the dough by lining the crust with parchment paper and filling with pie weights or raw rice (about 3 cups). Push the weights gently up the sides of the parchment, and bake for 20 minutes. Carefully remove the parchment and weights. Prick the bottom of the crust with a fork, return it to the oven, and bake for 10 to 20 minutes more, until the crust is golden brown and nearly done. Remove from the oven and let cool while you prepare the filling.

In a medium saucepan over medium heat, cook the Vanilla Sugar (or the regular sugar; you'll add the vanilla extract later), evaporated milk, 1 cup water, and the cornstarch, whisking continually, until the sugar melts. Whisk in the cocoa powder and ginger until they are combined.

Temper the egg yolks by placing them in a small bowl and stirring in 2 tablespoons of the hot cocoa mixture, 1 tablespoon at a time. Add the tempered eggs to the saucepan and cook, whisking, until the mixture thickens. Remove from the heat and whisk in the butter (and the vanilla extract, if using). Pour the filling into the cooled pie crust. Chill in the refrigerator for 2 hours.

Preheat the oven to 375°F.

To make the meringue, in a large mixing bowl with a hand mixer (or a stand mixer fitted with the whisk attachment), whisk the egg whites until soft peaks form. Whisk in the cream of tartar. Gradually whisk in the superfine sugar. Continue to whisk until the meringue is stiff and glossy. Top the chilled pie with the meringue, covering the pie filling to the edge of the crust to seal, then bake for 10 minutes, or until golden brown.

Weepy meringue? Because meringue has such a high sugar content and sugar is hygroscopic (meaning it absorbs moisture from the atmosphere), the humidity in a moist kitchen can cause your meringue to weep. This is especially noticeable on a very humid day. One way to avoid too much weeping is to add the sugar very gradually to the egg whites, making sure it is thoroughly incorporated after each addition, since undissolved sugar can attract moisture. The best answer is, of course, to eat the pie right after the meringue is browned. Then you don't have to worry about anything but a chocolate-covered face.

Pie Dough Scrap Shortcake

hillbilly napoleon | dessert | serves 4

Never throw away pie dough scraps . . . ever.

1 quart strawberries, rinsed, hulled, and quartered

3 tablespoons Vanilla Sugar (page 167)

½ recipe Way Better Than Basic Pie Dough,
for single-crust pie (page 167),
or frozen pie dough scraps (thawed)

½ cup cold whipping cream

Preheat the oven to 350°F. Line a baking sheet with parchment paper and set aside.

In a medium mixing bowl, combine the strawberries and 2 tablespoons of the Vanilla Sugar. Toss to coat, cover, and chill in the refrigerator until you are ready to use.

On a lightly floured surface, roll the dough out to ¼ inch thick. Cut the dough into 8 squares. Don't worry about the dough being cut perfectly—this is a country dessert, and the charm is in the mess. Put the cut pie dough on the prepared baking sheet and prick each piece with the tines of a fork. Bake for 20 to 30 minutes, until the dough begins to brown.

Using a hand mixer on medium speed, whip the cream in a large bowl until fluffy. Add the remaining Vanilla Sugar and whip until soft peaks form.

To assemble, place one piece of baked pie dough on a plate. Top with a generous spoonful of the strawberries. Cover with another layer of pie dough and top with a final layer of berries. Finish with a large dollop of whipped cream.

Anytime you make pie, save the scraps! Wrap them tightly with plastic wrap and put them in a zip-top bag in your freezer. In addition to Pie Dough Scrap Shortcake, the scraps also make a great last-minute cracker for serving with Old No. 7 Pâté (page 160) or Buttery Potted Ham (page 132).

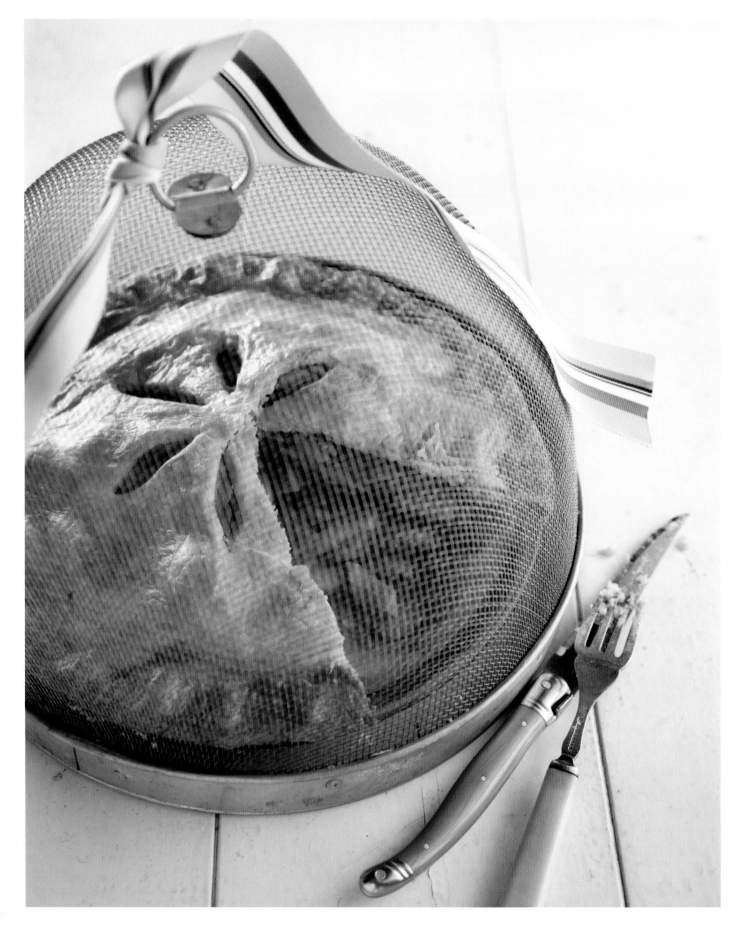

Blue Ribbon Apple Pie

apple butter and a kick | dessert | serves 8

I've been perfecting this pie for as long as I've been making it. When I was a child, it won me a third-place ribbon at the St. Charles County fair—just a step above the "participant" ribbon. I've convinced myself that if I were to enter today's recipe, it would be a blue-ribbon winner. Thus, I have awarded myself (and you) the prize here.

4 cups peeled and sliced Granny Smith apples (¼-inch slices)

4 cups peeled and sliced Pink Lady apples (¼-inch slices)

2 tablespoons freshly squeezed lemon juice

¾ cup prepared apple butter

1 tablespoon Vanilla Sugar (page 167)

6 tablespoons all-purpose flour

½ teaspoon ground cinnamon

¼ teaspoon ground cloves

Pinch of cayenne pepper

Way Better Than Basic Pie Dough, for double-crust pie (page 167)

2 tablespoons unsalted butter, cut into small pieces

1 large egg yolk

2 tablespoons milk

Preheat the oven to 400°F.

In a large mixing bowl, toss the apples with the lemon juice and apple butter.

In a separate mixing bowl, whisk together the Vanilla Sugar, flour, cinnamon, cloves, and cayenne. Sprinkle the sugar mixture over the apples and stir to coat. Set aside while rolling out the dough.

On a lightly floured surface, roll out one dough round into a 12-inch circle and drape it into a 9-inch pie plate, leaving a 1-inch overhang. Take care not to stretch the dough.

Fill with the apple mixture and dot the top of the apples with butter.

Roll out the second dough round to an 11-inch circle and drape it loosely over the top of the fruit (there will be defined peaks and valleys in the draped dough). Trim the edges of the dough and turn under at the outer edge of the pie plate rim, crimping the edges. Cut slits in the top of the pie to let steam to escape while the pie is baking. You may wish to decorate the pie crust with any remaining pieces of the dough.

Make an egg wash by beating the egg yolk together with the milk. Brush the crust with the egg wash, set the pie on a baking tray, and bake for 30 minutes. Lower the oven temperature to 350°F and continue to bake 30 to 35 minutes, until the crust is a dark caramel color and the fruit is bubbling around the edges and through the slits in the top. Let the pie cool for 30 minutes before serving.

Prodigal Chocolate Pig

white chocolate bacon rum sauce : dessert : serves 10 to 12

My favorite dessert, hands down. It's adapted from the classic Boca Negra, by Lora Brody. I have made it for years when working on private yachts, to the delight of guests and crew (one cake feeds everyone). All the original recipe needed was a bit of sow sass and some Bermudian pub logic—I've added them both.

½ cup Gosling's Black Seal Rum, or your choice of rum

1⅓ cups granulated sugar

12 ounces bittersweet chocolate, coarsely chopped

1 cup (2 sticks) unsalted butter, cut into 8 pieces, at room temperature

5 large eggs, at room temperature

2 tablespoons all-purpose flour

¼ teaspoon cayenne pepper

White Chocolate Bacon Rum Sauce (recipe follows)

12 chocolate candy pigs for garnish (optional)

Preheat the oven to 350°F. Grease a 9-inch round cake pan, line the bottom with parchment paper, and grease the paper. Set aside.

In a small saucepan over medium-high heat, combine the rum and sugar and bring to a boil.

Put the chocolate in a food processor fitted with the metal blade and pulse twice. Pour the boiling rum mixture over the chocolate and process until it is completely blended. With the processor running, add the butter one piece at a time. Add the eggs one at a time, processing well after each addition. Add the flour and cayenne and process for 20 seconds. Pour the batter into the prepared cake pan and smooth the top. Place the cake pan in a larger roasting pan and pour hot water into the roasting pan to a depth of 1 inch. Bake for 30 minutes.

Remove the cake pan from the water bath and wipe it dry. Let the cake cool for 5 minutes. Cover the top of the cake with plastic wrap and invert the pan onto a flat plate. Peel the parchment off the bottom of the cake before inverting it again onto a serving platter. Remove the plastic.

Serve the cake warm with a heaping spoonful of the White Chocolate Bacon Rum Sauce, garnished with chocolate pigs, if desired.

White Chocolate Bacon Rum Sauce

Yields 2 cups

1 cup heavy cream

1 pound white chocolate, chopped

¼ cup Gosling's Black Seal rum, or your choice of rum

4 slices bacon, cooked crisp, finely diced

In a small saucepan, heat the cream to a low boil.

Put the white chocolate in a food processor fitted with the metal blade and pulse once. Pour the simmering cream over the white chocolate and process until it is completely smooth. Add the rum and process until thoroughly combined. Remove the blade and stir in the bacon. Pour the sauce into a container with a tight-fitting lid and refrigerate overnight.

a parting gift

Massepain Trois Petits Cochons (Marzipan Three Little Pigs)   serves 3 to 6

Marzipan is a moldable and edible paste made from almonds and sugar. It is customary in Germany, Norway, and Denmark to give the gift of a marzipan pig to bestow good luck and fortune on your friends. Please consider these Massepain Trois Petits Cochons my gift to you, friends old and new, who are enjoying my little pig cookbook.

1 Pinch off a small piece of marzipan (about the size of a gumball) and set it aside (this is to make the berets). Wear gloves if you mind getting your hands stained. Work the large piece of marzipan into a ball, kneading it to soften. Using your finger, make a well in the middle and add 1 drop of pink food coloring gel. Start with just a small drop; you can always add more. Work the color into the marzipan by kneading the marzipan back and forth between your hands. Set aside. Now, working with the small ball of marzipan, add a drop of black food coloring gel and work the coloring in the same way. Set aside.

2 Pinch off a 2-inch ball from the pink colored marzipan and set aside for the feet, ears, and tail of each pig. Divide the remaining pink marzipan into 3 equal pieces and mold each into the shape of a jug. These will become each pig's snout and body.

3 Using a clay molding tool, press two holes in each pig's snout to make his nostrils.

4 Pinch off four small balls from the leftover pink marzipan and press them into the underside of one pig's body for his feet. Use the tip of a bamboo skewer to make a notch in the front two feet. Repeat on the other two pigs.

5 Pinch off two pea-size pieces from the leftover pink marzipan. Press each piece into a small circle and pinch each end together to make the ears. Press these ears into the top of the pig's head. Repeat on the other two pigs.

6 Pinch off a very small piece of the leftover pink marzipan and roll it into a tail. Coil the tail and press it into the butt of the pig to attach. Repeat on the other two pigs.

7 Press two blue dragées into one pig's face for eyes. Repeat on the other two pigs.

8 Divide the black marzipan into three pieces and mold three small French berets by shaping a flat disk around the tip of your forefinger. Place the berets between the ears on all three pigs.

9 Massepain Trois Petits Cochons! Share your pigs with friends. The sweet creamy marzipan in one pig alone is enough to satisfy the sweet tooth of two . . . or three . . . or even four people. May you all be happy, healthy, and prosperous.

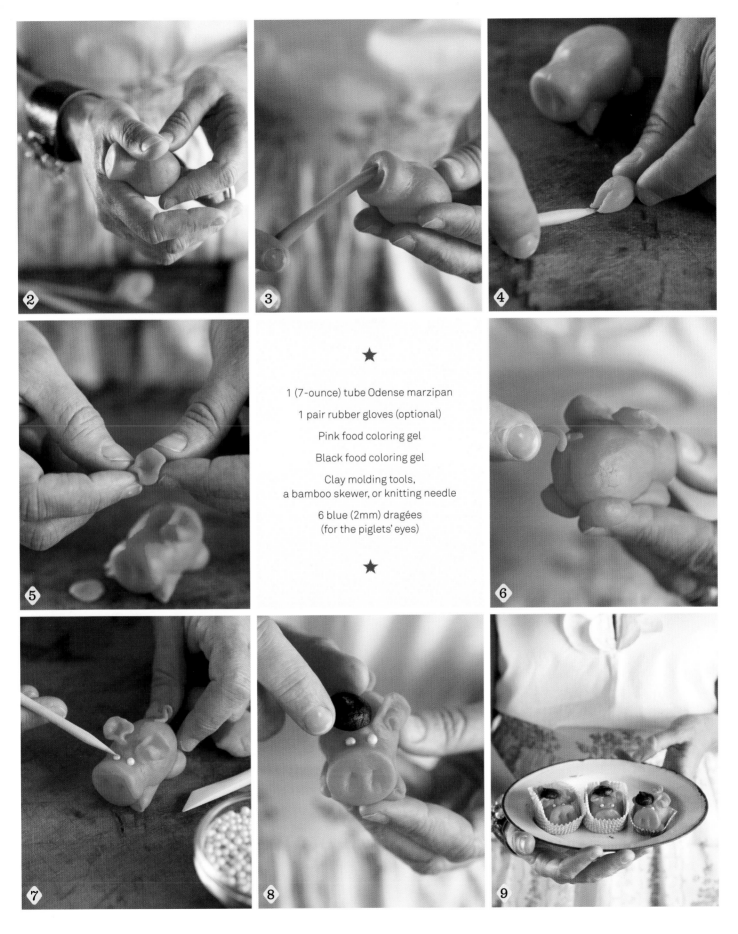

1 (7-ounce) tube Odense marzipan

1 pair rubber gloves (optional)

Pink food coloring gel

Black food coloring gel

Clay molding tools,
a bamboo skewer, or knitting needle

6 blue (2mm) dragées
(for the piglets' eyes)

Hog Resources

National/Online Retailers

Fromthefarm.com
800.930.3615
www.fromthefarm.com
*Online farmers' market retailer (no storefront);
allows customers to buy products directly from
several farms*

Heritage Pork International
712.202.2357
206 First Street
Sergeant Bluff, Iowa 51054
www.heritagepork.com
*Storefront and online orders; Heritage Berkshire
pork; humane, antibiotic and hormone free*

Igourmet.com
877.446.8763
www.igourmet.com
Online retailer only; organic Berkshire pork

Local Harvest
831.515.5602
P.O. Box 1292
Santa Cruz, California 95061
www.localharvest.org
*Online retailer only; several farms sell their
meat products through this website*

MeatHub
877.336.9482
15760 143rd Avenue Southeast
Renton, Washington 98058
www.meathub.com
*Online retailer; offers pâté, chops, ribs, ham,
loin, sausages*

Organic Prairie
877.662.6328
www.organicprairie.com
*Online retailer only; organic co-op of various
farmers from Iowa and Wisconsin*

Prime Chops Specialty Meats & Seafood
619. 222.0174
2538 East 53rd Street
Huntington Park, California 90255
www.primechops.com
Offers online organic mail orders

Savory Spice Shop
888.677.3322
various locations nationwide
www.savoryspiceshop.com
Alderwood-smoked salt

Smithfield
800.926.8448
Various locations nationwide
www.smithfield.com
www.smithfieldhams.com
www.smithfieldmarketplace.com
*Hams, bacon, sausages, and various pork
products available at Smithfield retailers, or
online; check the websites for locations*

William's Pork
910.608.2226
1027 U.S. Highway 74 East
Lumberton, North Carolina 28358
www.britishbacon.com
*Online retailer; specializes in British back bacon,
sausages, hams*

Zingerman's Food by Mail
888.636.8162
422 Detroit Street
Ann Arbor, Michigan 48104
www.zingermans.com
Mail-order food retailer; source for guanciale

South/Southwest

**Georgia's Texas Grassfed Beef
(and Natural Meats)**
979.921.0000
14182 Cochran Road
Waller, Texas 77484
www.texasnaturalmeat.com
*Natural pork (no growth enhancers, no
antibiotics, no chemical preservatives); available
by online order or store visit*

Rudolph's Market & Sausage Factory
214.741.1874
2924 Elm Street
Dallas, Texas 75226
www.rudolphsmarket.com
*Producing a variety of homemade sausages
for over a hundred years*

Southeast

Boutwell Farms
334.649.7690
1068 County Road 67
Clayton, Alabama 36016
www.boutwellfarms.com
*Online orders only delivering to Alabama,
Georgia, and Florida locations; natural pig
habitat and diet*

Butcher's Choice of Atlanta
770.446.3555
1710 Wilwat Drive Northwest
Norcross, Georgia 30093
www.butcherschoice.com
Online store

Caw Caw Creek Farms
803.917.0794
709 Woodrow Street #220
Columbia, South Carolina 29205
www.cawcawcreek.com
Heirloom pastured pork

Hickory Nut Gap Farm
828.628.1027
57 Sugar Hollow Road,
Fairview, North Carolina 28730
www.hickorynutgapfarm.com
Pasture-raised pork

J. B. Hendry
888.361.4574
6003 North 54th Street
Tampa, Florida 33610
www.jbhendrysteaks.com

West/Northwest

Don & Joe's Meats
206.682.7670
85 Pike Street
Seattle, Washington 98101
www.donandjoesmeats.com
Storefront in Pike Place Market

Drewes Bros. Meats
415. 821.0515
1706 Church Street
San Francisco, California 94131
www.drewesbros.com
Providing natural, free-range meats since 1889

The Fatted Calf Charcuterie
707.256.3684
The Oxbow Public Market
644 C First Street
Napa, California 94559
www.fattedcalf.com
Organic, hormone-free; sausage

Golden Gate Meat Company
415.851.3800
550 Seventh Street
San Francisco, California 94103
www.goldengatemeatcompany.com
*Storefront and mail order available; Berkshire
pork, Natural Hill pork, offal, cured meats,
sausage*

Hearst Ranch
866.547.2624
5 Third Street, Suite 200
San Francisco, California 94103
www.hearstranch.com
Ham, sausage, loin

Little Sprouts Farm
541.826.4345
4446 Dodge Road
White City, Oregon 97503
www.littlesproutsfarm.blogspot.com
*Online orders available by half, whole, or quarter
hog; organic, grass-fed, natural-foraging,
humanely raised Heritage pork*

Niman Ranch
1600 Harbor Bay Parkway, Suite 250
Alameda, California 94502
www.store.nimanranch.com
Crown roast, charcuterie

Salumi Artisan Cured Meats
206.223.0817
309 Third Avenue South
Seattle, Washington 98104
www.salumicuredmeats.com
*Guanciale (jowl) sausage, salami, cured shoulder,
cured loin*

Sweet Briar Farms
541.683.7447
28475 Spencer Creek Road
Eugene, Oregon 97405
www.sweet-briar-farms.com
*Hormone and antibiotic free; leaf lard, ribs,
roasts, hams, sausages*

Midwest

Angel Acres Farm
888.207.6903
60500 Maple Ridge Road
Mason, Wisconsin 54856
www.angelacresfarm.net
*Pasture-raised pork; orders can be placed by
phone, e-mail, or postal mail, or customers
may visit the farm*

Fiedler Family Farms
812.836.4348
14056 East State Road 66
Rome, Indiana 47574
www.fiedlerfamilyfarms.com
*Pasture-raised pork available for order by
phone, e-mail, or customers may visit the farm*

Franciscan Family Farms
573.200.6328
www.franciscanfamilyfarms.com
*Online orders can be picked up at the farm, or
special shipping arrangements can be made prior
to ordering; naturally raised Heritage breeds*

Gepperth's Market
773.549.3883
1964 North Halsted
Chicago, Illinois 60614
www.gepperthsmarket.com
Storefront retailer, online orders available for shipping via FedEx; variety of pork cuts, as well as a huge selection of specialty sausages

Good Earth Farms
888.941.4343
10431 Mayflower Road
Milladore, Wisconsin 54454
www.goodearthfarms.com
Pasture-raised, certified organic shoulder, loin, ribs, chops, Boston butt roast, shoulder roast

La Quercia
515.981.1625
400 Hakes Drive
Norwalk, Iowa 50211
www.laquercia.us/home
Prosciutto

Moo & Oink
773.420.2000
4100 40th Street,
Chicago, Illinois 60632
www.home.moo-oink.com
Some products available through online store (chitterlings, sausages, rib tips); several locations in the Chicago area

Paulina Meat Market
773.248.6272
3501 North Lincoln Avenue
Chicago, Illinois 60657
www.paulinameatmarket.com
Storefront or online orders; pork, sausage, ham, deli items available

Peek-A-Boo Acres
877.334.3276
www.peekabooacres.com
Loin, chops, patties, spare and country ribs, sausage, bacon, ham hocks

East/Northeast

Applegate Farms
888.587.5858
750 Route 202 South, Suite 300
Bridgewater, New Jersey
08807-5530
www.applegatefarms.com
Organic deli meats, sausages, hams, bacon

The Butcher Shop
617.423.4800
552 Tremont Street
Boston, Massachusetts 02118
www.thebutchershopboston.com
Storefront only; offers Berkshire pork, as well as pig's feet, pig head, and more

The Chitlin Market
P.O. Box 277
Hyattsville, Maryland 20781
www.offalgreat.com
Online retailer; hand-cleaned chitterlings (chitlins)

D'Artagnan
800.327.8246
280 Wilson Avenue
Newark, New Jersey 07105
www.dartagnan.com
Online retailer

Faicco's Pork Store
212.243.1974
260 Bleecker Street
New York, New York 10014
Famous butchery in the West Village

Fleisher's Grass-Fed & Organic Meats
845.338.6666
307 Wall Street,
Kingston, New York 12401
www.fleishers.com
Storefront in Kingston; New York City delivery available; local farms; hormone and antibiotic free, grass-fed

Florence Prime Meat Market
212.242.6531
5 Jones Street
New York, New York 10014
West Village storefront

Flying Pigs Farm
518.854.3844
246 Sutherland Road
Shushan, New York 12873
www.flyingpigsfarm.com
This farm sells at New York City farmers' markets and also will ship nationwide.

Heritage Foods USA
718.389.0985
402 Graham Avenue
Brooklyn, New York 11211
www.heritagefoodsusa.com
Retail; offers almost every cut, including trotters, ears, tail, back fat, and more

John Dewar & Co., Inc. Quality Meats
508.638.7700
1100 Pearl Street
Brockton, Massachusetts 02301
www.johndewarinc.com
Two storefront locations (Wellesley and Newton) and a wholesale office (Boston-Brockton); preorder for pickup is available

Lobel's Butcher Shop
877.783.4512
1501 East Avenue, Suite 210
Rochester, New York 14610
www.lobels.com
Storefront retailer; online orders available; Berkshire pork, a variety of sausages including andouille, Italian, kielbasa

O. Ottomanelli & Sons
212.675.4217
285 Bleecker Street
New York, New York 10014
www.wildgamemeatsrus.com
Famous for homemade chemical-, hormone-, and antibiotic-free sausages; in business since 1935

The Sausage Maker Inc.
888.490.8525
1500 Clinton Street, Building 123
Buffalo, New York 14206-3099
www.sausagemaker.com
Casings

SpitJack
800.755.5509
268 Boston Turnpike,
Shrewsbury, Massachusetts 01545
www.spitjack.com
Electric spit for roasting

Surry Farms
888.901.4267
P.O. Box 25
11455 Rolfe Highway
Surry, Virginia 23883
www.surryfarms.com
Order online or by phone or mail; pasture-raised, certified humane, antibiotic, and hormone-free Berkshire pork

Tide Mill Organic Farm
207.733.2551
91 Tide Mill Road
Edmunds, Maine 04628-5500
www.tidemillorganicfarm.com
Organic farm; offers cuts and whole sides of pork

Supplies

Habersham Antiques Market
912.238.5908
2503 Habersham Street
Savannah, Georgia 31401
www.habershamantiquesmarket.com
Vintage props

Le Creuset
877.273.8738
various locations nationwide
www.lecreuset.com
Cookware

Meddin Studio
912.944.6111
2315 Louisville Road
Savannah, Georgia 31415
www.meddinstudios.com
Studio space

Paula Deen Enterprises
912.644.3600
2391 Downing Avenue
Savannah, Georgia 31404
www.pauladeen.com
Studio space and time off from work

ReThink Design Studio
912.236.3022
114 West Jones Street
Savannah, Georgia 31401
www.rethinkdesignstudio.com
Interior architectural design

Satchel
912.233.1008
311 W. Broughton Street
Savannah, Georgia 31401
shopsatchel.com
Custom leather handbags

ShopSCAD
912.525.5180
340 Bull Street
Savannah, Georgia 31401
www.shopscadonline.com
Handmade jewelry

Star Bikes
912.927.2430
127 East Montgomery Crossroads
Savannah, Georgia 31406
www.starbikesavannah.com
Restored antique bikes

Living Libbie is good living! I love my life; family, friends and the ridiculously creative people I'm blessed to work with every day. This, my first personal book project, is a testament to all the creative people I surround myself with. I could fill an entire second book with accolades for some of the best people in this industry. Sadly, I only have this space to brag on them. Here goes!

Chia Chong, photographer. Thank you, Chia... my friend. Your talent and your heart shine from every page of this book. I will forever be your cheerleader.

To Paula, Jamie, and Bobby Deen. For opening the door and letting me run through. It is an honor and a pleasure to work for and with you. I always knew work could be fun. I just never knew it could be this fun. I adore you all.

To Rizzoli Publications for embracing this "pork for chicks" book and making it so beautiful.

To Christopher Steighner, senior editor, thank you for your endless thoughtfulness and ability to patiently wait until I finished talking.

To Don Chandler, Eric Esch, and the folks at Smithfield for always being so supportive of me and my work. Happy 75th Anniversary!

Jennifer Muller, designer. Thank you, Jennifer, for just getting it! For stepping in and giving my baby life and a new outfit. And for not hesitating a second when I said the orange needs to be more like an Hermès box orange.

Janice Shay, editor and book packager. Thank you, Janice! There would be no Whole Hog Cookbook if it were not for your negotiating skills and editing perseverance. I can't wait for our next project!

To heritage breed farmers Emile DeFelice and Eufren Ninancuro of Caw Caw Creek Farm in St. Matthews, SC. Thank you for providing a choice.

In styling all the shots, as well as formulating the design ideas, I was supported by Brooke Atwood, Michelle White, Lynn Rahn, Nathan Jones, Jules De Jesus, Tiffony Simpson, Jamie Cribbs, Mark Geary, Keith Rein, Sarah Meighen, Yiming Low, The Zucher Family, Joel and Erika Snayd, Evan Russell, and Hollis Johnson. My heartfelt thanks to you all.

Thanks and kisses to...
My dry-witted and hysterical son, Anthony, for graduating from Chapel Hill and still being willing to wash dishes on photo shoots. I am so very proud of you.
My dear friend, Brenda Anderson, your talent in the kitchen, laughter, and your light lifted me up when I needed it most. You amaze me.
My stylish BFF, Sydney Kiefner, for asking me every day how the book was going and reminding me to keep my eye on the prize.
My parents, for taking me to my grandparents' farm to ride the pigs. I love you both so very much.
My beautiful sisters, Robbie and Debbie: All the wonderful childhood memories include you.
My assistant, Jessica Miller, for keeping me organized and coffee fueled.
My friend and mother-in-law, Peggy, for your selfless support of everything I create.

Thank you to Virginia Willis, Johnnie Gabriel, and Melissa Clark for your mentorship and support.

Andrea Goto, manuscript editor. Thank you, Andrea, for making sense out of my writing, and cleaning up my language enough for everyone to enjoy. You are my literary hero.

To the most important person in my life, my husband, confidant, counselor and best friend, Josh. The way you have stood by me and held me up during this project has made me fall in love with you all over again. I will forever be in awe of your intellect, your joie de vivre, and your abs. I love you.

Heritage Breeds

Berkshire
This, the most popular of the heritage breeds, yields a bright pink meat that is sweet and creamy with a hint of nuttiness.

Duroc
A hearty and somewhat aggressive breed. Duroc pork is known for its high moisture content and rich flavor.

Gloucestershire Old Spot
A critically rare breed with a gentle temperament. Gloucestershire pork is known for its higher fat ratio that adds a juicy rich flavor.

Hereford
Resembling a Hereford cow in markings, these pasturing pigs have a calm disposition. They are slow growing, yielding a richly marbled and colored meat.

Large Black
A critically rare pasturing pig with wide shoulders and a long body. Its short muscle fibers and ample bellies produce moist meat and exceptionally tasty bacon.

Ossabaw
A rare breed of small-range pigs with a heavy coat and long snout. This breed has a high percentage of healthy fat and darker red meat that makes some of the best charcuterie.

Mangalitsa
Known as the "Wooly Pig" for its wooly coat and hearty disposition. This breed is known for its high-quality lard-like fat and super juicy, flavorful meat.

Red Wattle
Gets its name from the red color of its coat and the fleshy skin that hangs under its jowls. Prized for its tender meat with a rich beef-like taste and texture.

Yorkshire
The pigs of my youth! Yorkshires are hearty pasturing hogs and the females make wonderful mothers farrowing large litters of piglets.

Tamworth
A smaller athletic hog with a reddish coat and an ample belly. Tamworths produce the very best bacon.